SURVIVING

Hurricane María

September 18, 2017

Dedicated to my sweet wife Carmen, and
Hurricane María survivors everywhere.

By

M.D.Renicker

SURVIVING
Hurricane María

Index of Chapter Titles

***

SURVIVING
Hurricane Maria

INTRODUCTION

***

To write this account for you has been to relive each moment recounted herein: the joys, the heartaches, the horrors, and the love. It has therefore been, in roughly equivalent measures, one of the greatest honors and one of the greatest challenges of my life. I want to personally thank each of you for your interest in this tale of life and love and survival—a true series of wonderful and terrible events indelibly inked onto our hearts. As you walk through these experiences together with my lovely wife Carmen and me, you will find yourself openly invited into our hearts and homes in a way that becomes more personal with each page that you turn. This revealing portal into our lives is intentional, though I will admit that at times the transparency has been difficult to allow. Elements of this brutally honest portrayal of our experiences, shared from my perspective, have laid bare some of our deepest feelings and most intensely powerful emotions, leaving us rather vulnerable and exposed. My goal has been to share with you the most real, tangible, palpable experience mere words can offer, remaining as wholly authentic and accurate in the details as my memory allows. For completeness, I begin this anecdote in the early stages of medical school applications, to help you understand more fully the journey that led me to choose Ross University School of Medicine and end up on the Caribbean island of Dominica during one of the greatest and most fearsome storms to ever torture the face of the earth. So please, without further ado, join us in this partly beautiful, partly horrifying, and ultimately epic adventure of a lifetime.

***

SURVIVING
Hurricane Maria

Chapter 1:

The Discovery and the Decision

***

The sheets of gentle summer rain peacefully pelting the aged panes of my home-office window splattered in mesmerizing patterns across the uneven glass that had seen countless such showers in decades long gone. The tiny, scattered droplets would hover for a moment, as if developing a plan, and then quickly combine into larger and heavier droplets, trickling and dancing their way downward along the path that paradoxically seemed both choreographed and spontaneously created. The roll of distant thunder stirred me from my reverie. I needed to finish the email. Leaning forward to reach for the lever on my pesky office chair, I raised it a little too high in a futile attempt to compensate for the annoying way it self-lowered over time, pinching my legs a bit as I scooted closer to my desk. Glancing through the brief paragraph I had already written, I felt that the formal, awkward sentences seemed hollow, like the cliché husks of the words I wanted to say, but without true substance. The secondary application was complete and already attached to the email, and I was simply trying to find one final way to draw aside the curtain of technology and speak directly to the medical school admissions committee via an email message that would arrest their attention. This was the final of several secondary applications I had submitted that day, and the seemingly endless effort to create fresh, vibrant, new perspectives for each application was beginning to tax my creativity. How could I effectively reveal to medical school admissions committees who I really was in just a few short sentences? How could I show them what I would be capable of accomplishing? How could I fit the

SURVIVING
Hurricane María

full scope and urgency of my long-term vision and goals concisely into the final words of the email? Taking a deep breath, I closed my eyes for a moment and prayed, asking God for wisdom and clarity of mind.

***

The journey had already been a long one. Growing up in Alaska, I was fortunate to have parents who insisted on a quality elementary and high school education. As a result, my GPA, along with my GED and SAT scores, opened the doors to virtually any undergraduate university to which I wished to submit an application. Instead of going to college immediately after graduating from high school in 2004, however, I moved to China for about 2 years, where I studied Mandarin Chinese at a small university in Beijing and helped with various mission and humanitarian projects. The experiences of those 2 years would fill a book of their own, but suffice it to say that the multi-cultural influences on my life impacted me deeply, forever altering my perceptions of the world at large and filling me with deep gratitude for the blessing of being born a citizen of the United States of America. Of course, I have occasionally pondered the different directions my life might have taken, had I chosen to go to college directly after high school, rather than living in Asia for a couple of years. However, I have never really questioned the purpose of God's plan to use that time and those experiences to help shape me into who I am, nor have I doubted the value imparted to my life as a result of the exposure to such cultural diversity. I left Asia and returned to the United States in the summer of 2006 to begin my undergraduate education in Washington State, feeling drawn into some type of role in the medical field, though I could not clearly define what that role might be, at that time.

SURVIVING
Hurricane Maria

Shortly after returning to the United States, I was involved in an automobile accident, and though my injuries were relatively minor, my undergraduate education was delayed for a few more years. During this time, between 2007 and 2009, I met and married Carmen, about whom there are not enough spaces on all the bookshelves of the world to contain the volumes of admiration I could write. Never could I have imagined the blessing and support and rock she would become in my life. By the time I eventually returned to complete my undergraduate degree at Eastern Washington University (EWU) in 2010, my vision and calling had snapped more clearly into focus. By the end of my second year at EWU, I declared my "Biology, Pre-Med" major, and diligently pursued my clarified dream of practicing as a physician.

***

"Ba-ding!" The familiar chime of an incoming email interrupted my meditation. A quick glance at the subject line told me that it was from one of the medical schools I was interested in attending, so I clicked on the email, hoping to see the coveted word "Accepted" in the first few lines. As had been the case for some weeks, however, it was merely another email confirming the receipt of my transcripts, my letters of recommendation, or some other part of my application. "We appreciate your application and will contact you with a decision soon," the email said. I heaved a tired sigh, and then immediately felt a little guilty, realizing that I should be thankful that at least I was still being considered. After all, a friendly "not yet" affords a great deal more hope than a definitive "no." Returning to the draft of my email, I once again considered what I might say that would potentially intrigue the minds of the admissions committee. "Who are they? What

SURVIVING
Hurricane María

might their interests be?" I wondered. Obviously, I assumed they would be interested in things related to medicine and science, but that did not effectively narrow it down, much. I considered writing more about my extensive research experience. The research project had grown into far more than I would have dared to hope during my senior year at EWU, and the first phase was finally completed in the early summer of 2015. We were excited to share our results, which I was preparing to present at the October 2015 Society for Neuroscience convention in Chicago, IL. However, I had not actually presented yet, nor had we published the results, even though we tentatively planned to do so as soon as we could put together a manuscript. Feeling like that was a wealth of potential that was regrettably untappable for me at that moment, I typed a few brief lines focusing on my experiences with cultural diversity, and then hit "Send" on the email. Just like that, another secondary application had been submitted. Just like that, there was nothing more for me to do but wait and pray.

***

I was working full-time, in addition to preparing for my upcoming research presentation at the Society for Neuroscience convention, but I was still breathlessly awaiting the first acceptance letter from a medical school. Candidly, I was a little surprised by what seemed to me to be a delay in responses from medical schools. It was not as if I expected university faculty to jump up and down with delight upon receipt of my application, or fight over who had the best position to offer me. At least, I would never have described my expectations that way; but I did sincerely believe I had a reasonable resumé, valuable life experience, decent MCAT scores and an unusual degree of cultural diversity

SURVIVING
Hurricane María

in my personal history. I spoke in cliché humility to my wife and friends, saying I would just wait for God to open the door and then be happy with whatever options became available. However, I truly felt as though I would hear back very quickly from most, if not all of the medical schools to which I had applied, and would likely be accepted into enough programs to allow me a selection from which to choose. As I was beginning to see, by this point in the application process, things were not going to turn out exactly that way. Days turned into weeks, weeks turned into months, and still, I heard nothing from medical schools, beyond generalized reassurances that they were reviewing my applications. I was baffled. What was missing from my application? If nothing was missing, what was wrong with my application? If nothing was missing and nothing was wrong with my application, then why was I not being accepted? In retrospect, I understand much more about the sheer numbers of applicants and the quality of the competition, and I chuckle a little at my own naivety. In truth, I was nothing special; nothing out of the ordinary, with respect to the tens of thousands of other highly qualified medical school applicants competing in my application cycle. At the time, however, I was beginning to struggle with self-doubt and discouragement after a few months of silence. When the application deadlines passed, I felt as though I had done everything I could to improve my odds of earning an acceptance into a medical program. Thankful to have a diversion, I poured myself into my work and my research, always listening for the chime of the incoming email I so desperately wanted to receive.

***

The man seated next to me on the first leg of my flight to the October 2015 Society for Neuroscience convention in Chicago, IL, was a broad-shouldered man with a weathered face and heavily calloused hands. However, the calloused knuckles were paled by the man's tight grip on his armrest, and beads of sweat glistened on his brow as our plane was pushed back from the gate. In an attempt to distract him from his apparent fear of flying, I asked him where he was headed. "Mexico," he replied, through clenched teeth. "Oh, nice!" I said, and then pressed a little further. "Vacation or business?" He immediately brightened, even smiling a bit as he said, "A wedding—my daughter is getting married there." His grip had visibly loosened, and he seemed more relaxed after taking his mind off of his fears regarding his present circumstances, so I continued my conversation with him and enjoyed a pleasant flight with a friendly acquaintance. As I reflected on the event later, I was impressed by the parallels that could be drawn between that event and my own life circumstances. I had fully expected to be accepted to medical school before the fall Society for Neuroscience convention, and I was feeling increasingly stressed and concerned about the potential ramifications of failing to earn an acceptance. Various medical schools had been maintaining contact with me, and none had officially sent me rejection letters, but I was feeling a heightened sense of urgency with each opportunity of ongoing communication. I realized that I was facing my own fear—rejection from medical schools—which was most likely unfounded, but this fear was potentially inhibiting the positive outcomes of my other responsibilities. I decided in that moment that I would attempt to take my eyes off of the crippling uncertainty of my immediate circumstances. Instead, I would focus on the long-term goal of becoming a physician, do my best with each opportunity that presented itself along the way, and trust that God had a plan to open the right doors at the right time to facilitate the dream He had given me. The presentation at the Society for Neuroscience convention went off without a hitch, and the response from the attendees was overwhelmingly positive. To make the experience even better, I was joined in Chicago by my wife Carmen, who provided specialized training for regional activities directors of a nationwide dementia-care organization. She was able to organize a business training event at a Chicago facility the same week of my presentation, so together we enjoyed delicious, Chicago-style deep-dish pizza, and long walks through the beautiful, fall-season cityscape. I returned to Washington State eager to pursue publication of our research, at the urging of many Society for Neuroscience colleagues. Due to the completely novel aspects of our research, however, my team and I decided to delay publication until we had established the next phase of the research, in order to further support our findings.

***

"Ba-ding!" It was the spring of 2016, and once again the familiar chime of an incoming email drew my attention. By this point in the medical school application cycle, I expected to see rejection letters, rather than acceptance letters. I did not know anyone who had been accepted to a medical school this late in the process, and I was almost dreading the words of rejection I was sure I would read. This email, however, was a game-changer. In a moment I will never forget, I opened the email and read my first letter of acceptance into a medical school program: "Congratulations! We are pleased to be contacting you to inform you of your acceptance into the medical education program at..." That was about as far as I read before I leaped from my chair with a shout of excitement, thankful to God for the open door to a suddenly brighter future. I was ecstatic and more than a little surprised, because I had begun mentally preparing for what seemed like an inevitable round of reapplications. Grabbing my phone, I immediately called and made a reservation at one of our favorite downtown bistros, so I could take Carmen out to celebrate. When she got home that evening, I had the acceptance letter printed and displayed in all its glory on the kitchen table for her to see when she walked in the door. The moment she saw it, she gave a little squeal, "Eeeeekkk! Is this for real?! You are officially going to medical school??" My face-splitting smile was answer enough. I kissed her on the cheek, grabbed my keys, and we headed out the door to enjoy the special evening. In truth, the letter was not from a university that was anywhere near the top of my preferred list. We were mostly celebrating the confirmation that, regardless of what I heard from other schools from that moment forward, I did in fact have a seat in a medical school with the September 2016 incoming class. The feeling of reassurance was most welcome. Over the next week or two, I received a number of other acceptance letters, and it felt as though the floodgates of opportunity had suddenly been opened, even if it was happening much later than I ever dreamed it might. I felt as though God wanted me to recognize two things, beyond a shadow of a doubt: 1) He was confirming that He certainly did want me to be a physician, and 2) He was showing me that it was going to be Him opening the doors to my future, regardless of my own perceived strengths, abilities or achievements. That was perfectly fine with me. In fact, I found it reassuring, recalling an old Bible verse my dad would occasionally quote: "If God is for us, who can be against us?" (Romans 8:31b, NIV)

***

SURVIVING
Hurricane Maria

Should I opt for a US-based school, simply to avoid the stigma associated with certain Caribbean-based international medical schools? Will any mild stigma actually impact my future in any way, if I perform well on the USMLE Step exams? I contemplated these questions, as I wrestled with my new-found problem: choosing the best possible option, based on a variety of interests, concerns and long-term ambitions. I had applied to some Caribbean medical schools on a bit of a whim, admittedly, but I was sincerely interested in the idea of an internationally-based medical education, assuming it was fully accredited and well-respected in the United States. As it turned out, one of the top Caribbean-based medical schools, Ross University School of Medicine (RUSM), was the second institution to send me a letter of acceptance, and immediately provided information regarding a full-tuition scholarship for which I seemed to qualify. I do not recall being explicitly told that I was certain to receive the scholarship, but it was my understanding, per my conversations with my advisor and other admissions faculty, that I was a perfect candidate and merely needed to submit the application. Carmen and I thought and prayed about the array of options, discussing the US-versus-Caribbean possibilities with friends and colleagues in the medical field, and seeking the counsel of those with more experience and relevant perspectives. Over and over again, the RUSM scholarship kept surfacing in conversations as a remarkably good and rare opportunity, and I will readily admit that the idea of living in the Caribbean for a year and a half was powerfully enticing to lovers of adventure like us. With only a few days to make a decision after receiving the letters of acceptance, I scoured the internet for information about Dominica, "The

Nature Island" of the Caribbean and the host island of RUSM. What I discovered nearly took my breath away. There were countless images of high, misty waterfalls above glassy pools; mysterious rivers running through dense, tangled rainforests; boiling lakes and steaming mineral baths on the flanks of towering, dormant volcanos; endless, colorful coral reefs; lonely, winding, sandy beaches, without a soul in sight. The distant little island of Dominica was already beginning to capture my heart and my imagination, and I had not yet even informed RUSM of my decision that they were to be my medical school of choice.

***

Chapter 2:

The Differences and the Dances

***

The weeks following the decision to attend RUSM were filled with the predictable flurry of activities related to an international move. Carmen and I discussed the possibility of her staying in the United States and retaining her employment, a position she had worked hard to earn and income that would be helpful while I was unemployed in medical school. However, we both agreed that after seven years of marriage, having weathered the normal ups and downs of life with a partner, we wanted to make every effort to ensure our lives were increasingly intertwined, rather than separated. "We've been married for seven years, and we do life together!" Carmen stated emphatically, with a calm, confident smile. I was impressed and humbled by the love revealed in her ready willingness to sacrifice her hard-earned position in management to follow me into the unknown challenges of medical school and temporary unemployment. Very soon after making our decision, we both submitted our thirty-day notices of resignation to our workplaces. Then, there were lists of immunizations, health check-ups and police records to obtain for immigration to Dominica, adding to the typical to-do lists that send new medical students scrambling. If we were not at a clinic waiting on a test result or immunization, Carmen and I were standing in line at the local police station to request letters of good conduct, or searching online for the medical supplies and equipment I was required to take to the island. Candidly, it was easy to temporarily lose sight of the goal—becoming a physician— while scrambling so madly to meet the basic requirements to begin the medical program, especially at a school that was on foreign soil. In the final four weeks before we left Washington State, we sold or gave away most of our belongings from our home there, including two of our cars. We kept only our trusty GMC Yukon SUV and the few items that would fit into the Yukon and the small rental trailer we intended to obtain. The plan was to load the rental trailer and the Yukon, and then drive east from Washington State to Virginia, taking our time and enjoying a few weeks of vacation along the way, before I plunged into the rigors of medical school. Carmen's parents had kindly offered us a storage space in Virginia to use until we returned from Dominica, establishing a convenient location from which we could travel to and from the island.

***

Sorting through our personal belongings basically occurred on three separate levels. Level 1 required us to determine what belongings would be absolutely crucial to take with us to the island,

SURVIVING
Hurricane Maria

which we limited to what we could fit into four suitcases, two carry-ons, and a fifty-gallon shipping container. Level 2 required us to determine what belongings we ought to keep in storage until we returned from Dominica, since we would need to set up another residence with relatively little time to make arrangements and purchase new household items. Level 3 required us to determine what belongings we simply ought to get rid of, quickly becoming the most challenging and the most freeing level of sorting. It was surprisingly challenging to let go of the many excess belongings we had almost inexplicably valued for so long; but it was incredibly freeing to fill truckload after truckload, some of which contained useful items we donated to local charities and some of which contained worn-out items we hauled to the city waste management facility. This little "exercise in letting go", as we later referred to it, was not limited to personal belongings, of course. My parents and siblings were in Washington State at that time, as well, and it was hard to imagine when we might see them again because many of the RUSM rotations seemed to be in the eastern half of the United States. My family had always been a rock for me—a safe place to share ideas, vent frustrations, and seek counsel. Their love and prayers for us were invaluable throughout my undergraduate years, and we knew the additional miles of separation would only make our priceless connections less frequent. Thankfully, we were able to enjoy a sweet time of bonding with my parents, my siblings and their families, just before heading east. Though it was intensely hard to let go of their warm hugs when we parted, we felt immensely blessed by their supportive love. There were also many wonderful friendships we had developed while living in Washington State, and we dreaded letting go of those close, reliable connections far more than we dreaded letting go of mere belongings. There were people like Kurt and Linda, to whom we had grown close through our connection at a local church, and with whom we felt a unique kind of bond that seemed much more familial than a mere friendship. Many others could be named as well, and surely deserve to be, were a list to serve as proof of our love and respect for them. We truly regretted that we would soon be separated from them by so many miles. Difficult though it may have been, at times, we mercifully had no idea how valuable this little "exercise" was going to be to us in the near future.

***

His shaky voice and the tears in his eyes belied his wavering, lop-sided smile. Goodbyes are never easy anyway, and this one promised to be one of the hardest. At 80-something years of age, our landlord and dear friend "Jim" had become one of my closest friends, allies and confidants. My respect for his dry humor, quick wit, profound wisdom and irrepressible optimism knew no limits, and I was finding it hard to imagine life without the regular, hour-long conversations with one of the greatest men of faith I have ever had the honor of knowing. I had learned a great deal from Jim during the years of our friendship, and I was certain I would miss him more than words could express. So, instead of saying "goodbye", when the time came for us to leave for the east coast, I gave Jim a hug, wished on him God's blessing, and told him I would look forward to seeing him again soon. There was not much more that I could say, with a voice that was cracking a little with emotion, but nothing more really needed to be said anyway. We both understood the feelings of a depth greater than words could justly communicate.

***

SURVIVING
Hurricane Maria

Finally, the Yukon and the rental trailer were both successfully packed. I say "successfully packed" because I have to admit that it took more than one attempt to get the weight appropriately distributed in the trailer. After the first attempt to get everything in, we had to empty and repack at least half of the contents of the trailer two more times, before we finally had a reasonable tongue weight on the trailer that would allow the Yukon to pull it safely at highway speeds. At last, however, I was able to slide the door shut and lock it securely. I stepped back to survey the Yukon-and-trailer caravan in the early light of the predawn morning, feeling both exhausted from the sleepless night and satisfied with the final results. Standing there for a moment lost in thought, I pondered the miles and weeks and years that lay ahead. In so many ways, it felt as though things were going to be different, from this point forward. It was hard to define specifically what would be different, or the ways in which those things would change; and yet, it seemed even harder to identify anything at all that would ever truly be the same. I was snapped back to reality by the gentle brush of a hand on my shoulder. Approaching softly and pressing close to my back, Carmen slipped her arms around my waist beneath my arms and, tilting her face upward, she rested her chin on the back of my shoulder, head cocked slightly sideways, studying the profile of my face with a tired smile. "It's really happening, isn't it, babe?" she asked, not waiting for an answer before continuing. "You are going to be a doctor...And I get to be a doctor's wife!" Her eyes sparkled in the early morning light, as she spoke. "It's like a dream..." she said, her voice trailing off as a glistening, silver tear trickled down to accent the radiant joy on her face. The first songbirds were beginning to serenade the pink and yellow rays of sunrise splashed across the

SURVIVING
Hurricane Maria

glowing sky. A gentle breeze stirred the cool morning air, tussling the leaves on the branches of the young apple tree standing next to us, and springing a tear to my own weary eye. Or, perhaps the breeze just coincided with the single tear that threatened to fall. Either way, the sweetness of the moment was kissed with perfection. Clasping Carmen's hands in mine, holding her tight against my back and tilting my face to rest my cheek against hers, I slowly started to sway as I whispered, "Would you like to dance a moment with me?"

***

We were somewhere in Colorado when the swaying of the trailer and the shudder from the rear of the Yukon became too extreme to ignore. Pulling into a rest area, I hopped out and asked Carmen to drive slowly forward in first gear while I walked alongside the Yukon and scanned for the cause of the poor drivability. "Whoa, that's far enough!" I called out to Carmen, who immediately stopped the vehicle after driving only a few feet. Something had caught my eye on the driver's side rear tire. Upon closer inspection, the problem was clear: one of the severe potholes in the last few miles of road construction had sliced the inner wall of the tire, and the steel bands were bulging outward in a way that made a burst tire seem inevitable. It was about 5:30 p.m., so I hurriedly searched online for a nearby tire shop that might still be open in the small town we were just entering. After a few phone calls, I finally found a shop within a few miles that reportedly closed at 6:00 p.m. Slowly inching my way along the road, praying the tire would not let go, we finally arrived at the tire shop around 5:50 p.m. Leaping from the Yukon and dashing into the store, I was less annoyed than I might usually have been by the sound of the clanging cowbell that hung from the inner doorknob and clattered raucously against the swinging front door, because it meant the unlocked door was swinging open for me. Laying aside a greasy newspaper, which appeared to be dated from some weeks earlier, the manager kindly welcomed us in and went directly to work. He may have been slow getting his news, but he was brilliantly efficient in the tire shop. An hour later, we were pulling away with four new tires, after deciding it would be best to replace them all, due to their age and relatively well-worn condition. To our immense relief, driving 70 mph on the freeway was perfectly smooth once again, and we thoroughly enjoyed the rest of our road trip east.

***

Once we arrived in Virginia, we quickly unpacked the rental trailer and returned it to the local rental agency, thankful for the dry and secure storage offered by Carmen's parents for our belongings. Because we arrived on the east coast a few weeks before our flight was scheduled to leave for Dominica, we enjoyed the extra time with family on that side of the United States, both in Ohio and in Virginia. In the interim, we reorganized and repacked our luggage and shipping container, repeatedly forced to downsize as we reached and exceeded the relevant weight and volume limitations. Informed that it would take at least two or three weeks for our shipping container to arrive in Dominica, we filled it with the less time-sensitive items and made the four-hour drive to Washington, DC, delivering it to the shipping company approximately one week prior to our flight date. It felt remarkably strange to be shipping a container full of our personal belongings to an island in the Caribbean we had never before seen. There was something strangely definitive about watching the container disappear down the shipping warehouse corridor, almost as if it was the final punctuation at the end of that chapter of life.

Now, it was even more official; we must go to the Caribbean because we would soon have a shipping container there waiting to be retrieved. On August 23, 2016, we said our goodbyes to family in Virginia and boarded our flight to the Caribbean. There were two layovers along the way, one in Florida and one in Barbados, and we enjoyed meeting a few of my new classmates who happened to be on the same flights. Upon arrival in Barbados, we were met just inside the terminal by RUSM personnel, who shuttled us quickly through customs and facilitated the check-in process for our final flight to Dominica.

***

"Is that it?" I excitedly asked Carmen, over the roar of the turbo-prop engines, pointing through the foggy airplane window toward a dark shape rising from the clouds in the distance. "You're worse than a two-year old," she laughed, "We just left Barbados ten minutes ago!" I will admit, I was almost vibrating with excitement. Well, excitement and caffeine; I am pretty sure the three cups of coffee I drank in Barbados were kicking in, as well. Speaking of the three cups of coffee I had just consumed, I was secretly beginning to feel a slight urgency to arrive in Dominica for more reasons that just my curiosity. Glancing back at the tiny door marked "Lavatory" at the rear of the plane, I was hesitant to attempt to fit even my average six-foot frame into it since it did not appear to be substantially larger than the coffee cups responsible for the concerns. Gritting my teeth, I loosened my seatbelt slightly in a vain effort to reduce bladder pressure, and turned my attention back to the foggy little window. Through occasional holes in the clouds, I could see the water of the Atlantic Ocean far below. I am not sure what I expected, really, but I was not overwhelmed by the views offered through the tiny portals. The glimpses of the ocean made it appear no different than any other ocean viewed from twenty-five thousand feet, with the typical dull-gray water and endless, tiny, rippling waves disappearing over the horizon. Though the tropical beauty of the islands and Caribbean Sea were hidden away from view, the miles of brilliantly white, towering clouds inspired awe in a beauty of their own. Just as I was reconsidering the possibility of using the tiny room at the back of the plane, the captain's voice sounded over the intercom: "Ladies and Gentlemen, please be sure your seatbelts are securely fastened, your seatbacks are upright, and your tray-tables are in their upright and locked positions. We will be landing in Dominica in just a few minutes." I forgot all about the call of the lavatory. Fogging the little window up even further, I wiped it down and strained to catch my first glimpse of the small island that would become our "home" for the next year and a half. Then, with the plane bursting down through the bottom layer of clouds, I finally saw it. I smiled. The beautiful little island of Dominica lay elegantly between the Atlantic Ocean and the Caribbean Sea, as if the crown jewel in a setting of unparalleled design. The rolling whitecaps of the Atlantic Ocean crashed and foamed over the rocky eastern shores of the island, while the mirror-like surface of the calm Caribbean Sea gently washed over miles of pristine beaches on the western shores. Perhaps most striking was the small size of Dominica, like a tiny paradise lost in the vastness of the surrounding bodies of water. Approaching the airport from the Atlantic side, we were quite low over the water before the single runway of the Douglas-Charles Airport sprang into view, and I was immediately thankful for the notably small size of our turbo-prop aircraft. The runway looked scarcely long enough for the plane to slow to a stop, from my perspective, but I trusted that the pilots knew what they were doing. I quickly forgot my concerns anyway, as I tried to snap a few pictures through the window with my cell phone, wishing with all my heart that I had remembered to grab my "real camera"—my digital SLR—from my carry-on in the overhead bin. Safely on the ground, the plane slowed almost to a stop and then gently performed a complete 180-degree turn in the middle of the runway to taxi back to the only accessible taxiway, offering my first real view of the airport. It could be viewed in its entirety without the slightest rotation of my head, as well, so tiny it was. The quaint little huddle of concrete and wooden buildings reminded me strongly of the small-town airports I had grown up seeing in rural Alaska. Squeezing Carmen's hand as we taxied toward the building that seemed to serve as the airport's only terminal, I winked and whispered so as not to be heard by my future colleagues, "Welcome home."

Stepping from the plane, I could see only a few other tiny cargo planes sitting on the tarmac that was so small it took less than a minute to traverse on foot. The wave of heat was noticeable, but not unbearable, as we made our way across the tarmac, though I did immediately break into a light sweat due to the intense humidity. We had our immigration paperwork in-hand, and followed the directives of the smiling airport staff as we made our way into the indicated building. There were no clear markings to guide us along, that I could discern, but the options were limited and the crowd seemed to be headed in the right direction. Once inside, the warm humidity of the tropical air was gently stirred by a few noisy fans, likely placed for the benefit of the two sleepy looking immigration agents who were perched behind desks at the front of meandering lines near the middle of the room.

SURVIVING
Hurricane Maria

They were stamping entry documents in a slow-but-steady, rhythmic manner, showing not even the least bit of concern for the legitimacy of the documents. Perhaps they were highly skilled, and would have readily recognized forged documents; or perhaps there actually was no need to be concerned, because Dominica really was that great and that safe. I felt inclined to think the latter was more likely to be true, but perhaps that was influenced by my die-hard optimism. I did not have long to ponder it, though, because we were soon through immigration, and found ourselves waiting on the other side of the immigration desks near a sloped shelf that was about ten feet long and four feet wide. At the back of this shelf was a roll-up steel door that we were informed would soon open to allow the delivery of our luggage. We waited, anxiously hoping our luggage had made it through with us, as reports from others indicated their luggage had not always arrived on the same flights. Exhausted from the long hours of travel, it seemed a little surreal to be standing in a superbly tiny airport on a Caribbean island that would be our home for the first two years of my medical education. Was this real life? Was I dreaming? Was I really seeing a coconut on the palm tree outside the window? Was I really going to live and study in this place for almost two years? Was I really ready, mentally and academically, for the intensity of the program I was about to start? I glanced around the room at the faces of my future colleagues; some smiled, some stared at the floor, some had their eyes closed, but all looked intelligent, confident and capable. I could not help but smile, feeling indescribably fortunate to be counted among such an impressive group of individuals. This was going to be an intensely amazing experience. I could feel it.

***

SURVIVING
Hurricane Maria

"*BUZZZZ! BUZZZZ! BUZZZZ!*"

The red light flashed at the end of the sloped luggage shelf. Someone outside the roll-up steel door firmly thumped on it a few times, presumably to knock loose any obstructing agents, such as excessive rust or wayward coconut shells, and then cranked it open. Sure enough, there was our luggage; and since there were only about fifteen other passengers who had arrived with us on our flight, there was no waiting in long lines. We simply picked up our baggage and walked away. We passed quickly by the smiling customs agents, who waved us on toward the exit door after only a few basic questions regarding the contents of the bags. "Are you carrying anything illegal? Are you carrying any fruit? Do you have anything else you would like to tell us about?" they asked. We responded with a cheerful "No" to each question, which seemed to fully satisfy their responsibility (or their curiosity—I was never really sure which, but it made no difference to me). With all of our luggage in tow, Carmen and I made our way out through the swinging doors, uncertain what we were looking for, but following the guidance of the friendly airport security staff. Outside, there was a general hubbub of cheerful chatter from the cluster of waiting taxi drivers, but we dashed their rising hopes when we turned toward the person holding a small sign: "Welcome, Students! (Ross University School of Medicine Shuttle Service.)"

***

Carmen had been gripping my hand so firmly for so long it had begun to tingle, as our small shuttle flew up the narrow, winding roads that led to the university. She grimaced apologetically when I laughingly tugged at my aching hand, and she immediately loosening her grip sufficiently to allow blood flow to resume. Although it was being used as a two-lane road, the narrow, paved track was just wide enough to allow two medium-sized vehicles to pass with merely inches between mirrors. To make matters more interesting, the traffic patterns were reversed, relative to those in the United States, with the drivers seated on the right side of the vehicles and the vehicles driving on the left side of the road. As we careened around hairpin turns, shot across one-lane bridges, and clawed our way—gears grinding—over the steep, volcanic mountains, I was enjoying every moment. Carmen quickly relaxed, and I could tell by the sparkle in her deep blue eyes that she, too, was enjoying the adventure. The lush rainforest rose immediately on either side of the roadway, with no shoulder or buffer that might have offered a degree of forgiveness for a mistaken movement of the steering wheel. The trunks of the swaying coconut palms were whisking by as closely on the one side as the mirrors of the passing cars were whisking by on the other. It did not seem to matter that there was not an inch to spare, though, as the local drivers effortlessly and artfully navigated passed one another at breathtaking speeds in a display of skillful driving that seemed almost choreographed. The machete-wielding farmers working the numerous banana farms waved and called out a friendly, "Yah, man!" as we passed. Cows and other livestock were tied with reed ropes to coconut palms along the roadway, with their owners apparently less concerned about the danger of the animals being struck by an automobile than the hassle of searching the dense jungle for them that evening. Groups of uniformed school children played along the streets in the little villages, flashing brilliantly white smiles, while their bouncing, black curls danced merrily. The buildings, from the small wooden huts to the large concrete apartment complexes, were all painted and brightly decorated in yellows, reds, greens, purples, pinks, and countless other brilliantly tropical colors. Even though it was midday, groups of local farmers and other villagers seemed to have nothing more important to do than lean against the wooden frame of the nearest "snackette", a small food shack, and chat and chuckle and curiously watch us pass by. Although the road across the island was inland, we were occasionally high enough in elevation to catch

fleeting glimpses of the Atlantic Ocean and the Caribbean Sea through breaks  in the dense wall of trees. Periodically, our driver would slow for a moment, scan each of our faces in the rearview mirror for signs of motion sickness, and ask how we were feeling. He was being very kind, even offering sprigs of lemon grass for us to chew, if we felt nauseated; but I had to wonder whether he was more concerned about our welfare, or his van's. Whatever his motives may have been, most people in our shuttle seemed generally OK, in spite of a few mildly green faces, so the driver always pressed on. After more than an hour of winding through the mountains, we finally broke from the rainforest and drove into Portsmouth and Picard, getting our first look at our new "hometowns." Admittedly, the towns were smaller than I might have imagined, and a bit more rustic, perhaps; but I had lived in Asia for two years, traveling extensively through the rural countryside while I was there, so I was not bothered by the basic simplicity of the environment.

There was no denying that it was beautiful. Nestled at the foot of towering, dormant volcanoes, Portsmouth and Picard wrapped around a small harbor on the edge of the calm, brilliantly blue Caribbean Sea. The harbor was dotted with dozens of colorful, wooden fishing boats, interspersed with the occasional sailing vessel or tourist's yacht. Sandy beaches could be seen in either direction, with

rock-flanked shipping docks stretching out into the clear, smooth sea like a  picture directly from a Caribbean advertisement. I caught Carmen looking at me with a dry smile, and I laughed. I did not need to say a word; she could plainly see I was already falling in love with the island.

***

"Welcome to Dominica!" said the cheerful "Welcoming Committee" volunteer from an upper semester. "Have a seat and enjoy your meals. We have contacted your landlords, and they should be here within the next half-hour to meet you and take you to your apartments." RUSM had provided a much-needed hot meal for us upon arrival at the RUSM Student Housing Department office, and we were already devouring the steaming dishes of chicken and rice with enthusiasm—so much enthusiasm, in fact, that we waited some time before trying the large cup of an unspecified type of yellow juice they also provided with our meals. When we did finally try a sip of the juice, however, Carmen's eyes sprang open wide in astonishment. "That's amazing!" she gasped, before taking the straw back in her mouth and draining the cup dry. I had to agree, the freshly made passion fruit juice was quite possibly the most deliciously refreshing tropical drink I had ever enjoyed. How much of our delight in the novel drink was due to our general delight in our novel environment may never be known, exactly; it is true, however, that passion fruit juice immediately earned a leading position on Carmen's short list of "favorite drinks", where it has unshakably remained ever since.

***

Leroy, our new island landlord, showed up right on time, just as we were finishing our satisfying meal. He was a tall, kind, local man with a gentle, easy-going personality that made us like him right away. Although he was a true islander through-and-through, he had lived in the United States for a period of time in his youth, and then served on the police force in Dominica for most of his career. His quiet strength and gentle mannerisms were reassuring to us, as we had been obligated to rent our apartment from him before arriving on the island and had some mild misgivings about what it would actually be like in-person. Much to our delight, it was precisely as advertised, and turned out to be a very comfortable apartment. It was early afternoon, so we immediately began unpacking the belongings from our suitcases, hoping to be somewhat settled early enough to find a restaurant with a view in time to watch the sunset. Our ambitions did not go unrewarded, and we were fully unpacked within a couple of hours. Throwing my camera bag over my shoulder, I followed Carmen out the door to do a little exploring. First, we stopped by RUSM Student Affairs to collect our campus identification cards, and then we went searching for a restaurant with a view. Just as the sun was dropping toward the horizon, we settled into a table at a quaint little restaurant on the edge of the Caribbean Sea. In front of the restaurant, an

old wooden pier stretched out into the bay, splitting the glowing

SURVIVING
Hurricane Maria

reflection of the brilliant orange and golden sunset on the gently rippling water. The silhouettes of several casually reclining people could be seen along the pier, and the finger-like shadows of the coconut palm leaves playfully danced on the sparkling waves that lazily lapped

at the sandy shores.  There were no seagulls, to our surprise, with the only audible bird calls being the distant screech of a parrot or the occasional splash of a diving pelican. The warm breeze blowing softly in from the sea lightly swept the white curtains decoratively separating different areas of the small restaurant, and the reggae-rhythm of local music drifted pleasantly from somewhere in the back. The seasoned chicken and fish dinner, served with lightly fried plantains, steamed vegetables and local juices, was cooked to perfection. Was it possible this was Heaven? I was standing for a moment at the railing, snapping a few pictures with my camera and taking in the indescribable beauty, when I felt a hand brush my shoulder. Approaching softly and pressing close to my back, Carmen slipped her arms around my waist beneath my arms and, tilting her face upward, she rested her chin on the back of my shoulder, head cocked slightly sideways, studying

the profile of my face with a tired smile. As I tilted my face to rest my cheek against hers, she slowly started to sway as she whispered, "Would you like to dance a moment with me?"

***

SURVIVING
Hurricane Maria

Chapter 3:

The Days and the Developments

***

Week one on the island was a nonstop blur of discovery and adventure. Everything about Dominica seemed unique in some way, and Carmen and I enjoyed the challenge of learning and adapting to our new environment. The traditional island greeting on the street, for example, was a friendly "Yah, man, I good. You good? Cool, cool, man." The accents were thick with "Patois" (French Creole) influence, the accompanying smiles were wide and sincere, and the dark eyes sparkled brightly from beneath the thick bundles of dreadlocks that seemed to be the hairstyle of choice on the island. It was considered impolite to pass even a stranger without at least a nod and a "Yah, man", and the locals often expressed their surprise and consternation over the way we foreigners seemed to frequently pass one another without so much as making eye contact. It was not uncommon at all to see two passing vehicles come to a complete stop in the middle of a busy roadway, with traffic screeching to a halt and stacking up in both directions, just so the drivers could call out their greetings to one another through their open windows. "Aaaayyyee, man! You good? You good? Cool, cool, man! Good seeing you! Yah, OK, OK, I'll be seeing you, man!" they might say, while the rest of the world—on that street, at least—simply waited. In complete contradiction to our North American attitude-conditioned expectations, the other local drivers on the road seemed to expect it, patiently tolerating the unpredictable delays. We loved it. There was something about it that was just so wholesome; it seemed authentic and community-oriented.

***

SURVIVING
Hurricane Maria

"BAM! BAM! BAM!" It was 11:30 p.m., and Carmen and I were already in bed. The banging on the front door brought me scrambling out of bed in search of a pair of pants. "Who is it?" Carmen whispered, as the mutter of voices drifted in from a small group of men outside our door. "I don't know," I replied, as I pulled on a shirt and headed out to see what the commotion was all about. Through the curtains on the front window, I could see four or five men milling around on our front steps, and a truck parked in the roadway. Opening the door, a cluster of smiling faces greeted me, as if they had no idea it was past a medical student's bedtime. "Hey, man, we've got your barrel!" they proudly announced, and I immediately forgave them for coming at such a crazy hour. "Fantastic," I replied, a little shocked that the shipping container had made the journey from the United States in little more than a week and a half. Digging in my wallet, I paid them for their exuberant services. They heaved the fifty-gallon container into the middle of our kitchen floor, and sputtered quickly off into the night in the smoking, coughing little flatbed pickup. It was like Christmas for Carmen and me—very much like Christmas, in fact, because even though we knew exactly what was in the container, having packed it ourselves, we still exclaimed with very real delight over each item.

***

Exploring the trails, towns, beaches and mountains with my camera in-hand was already becoming my new favorite pastime. The scenery was breathtakingly beautiful. Pristine rainforests, more lush and green than any I had ever seen, blanketed the dormant volcanos and mystically enshrouded the twisting rivers. A secret, white-sand beach, hidden away from the prying eyes of the world by towering cliffs of volcanic rock and accessible only by boat, was rumored to lie somewhere on the other side of a towering outcropping of rocks that jutted  imposingly out into the Caribbean Sea. An ancient fortress, replete with rows of heavy cannons dating back to the 1700s, begged to be explored from its perch on the shoulder of the Cabrits hills across the harbor. Even in the week of exploration before my medical school orientation began at RUSM, we hiked tens of miles, tried perhaps a dozen new restaurants and snackettes, and took hundreds of pictures. I posted so many pictures to social media, in fact, that I feared my friends might be growing weary of my images cluttering up

their newsfeeds. Perhaps a few did feel that way, but if so, they were all kind enough to at least pretend to be interested.

***

Walking back to our apartment one afternoon, we approached a man and a woman who were animatedly talking in the middle of the road. I wondered for a moment if we were walking up on a domestic dispute. The woman's face could not be seen, as her back was toward us, and she was much shorter than the broad-shouldered, stocky man. As she stood quietly listening, the man gestured wildly with his arms, his facial expressions taking over where his limbs were deemed inadequate, explaining something about a neighbor, a speargun and a monster barracuda. Nearing the couple on the narrow road, I opened my mouth to call out a friendly "hello", but was cut off by peals of laughter erupting from the woman, who doubled over in gleeful hysterics at whatever the man had just been saying, gasping out in a Texas drawl, "Daaaaaviiiddd...hahaha! That's too funny!" These two wonderfully delightful people introduced themselves as David and Chesley, and we immediately fell into conversation as if we had been friends for life. At one point during our lengthy chat in the middle of the street, I saw a rat clamber up out of a drain behind Chesley. I should clarify, at this point, that this was not just any rat. It was easily the largest rat I had ever seen, being much larger than the Sprague-Dawley rats with which I was familiar from my research back at EWU. This rat was huge. Uncertain how our new friends felt about positively enormous rats, but believing it safest to assume they might not respond favorably to this particularly mangy monster, I remained calm and said nothing. Watching the movements of the rat out of the corner of my eye, I carried on in conversation as if nothing was wrong, which was easier than it sounds since David was in the middle of another of his hilarious tales. The moment the rat scrambled back down a different drain on the other side of the road, I spoke up. "Guys...I just saw the largest rat I have ever seen." Carmen instantly grabbed my arm, eyes narrowing with suspicion, likely due to my tendency to attempt pranks that may have sounded somewhat similar in nature. "You saw what?" she asked, searching my eyes for the sparkle that might indicate I was joking. Chesley's eyes brightened, and she smiled as she cooed, "Awww, cute! Where did he go? I wanna see him!" We all laughed. "No, seriously guys, I wanna see him! Was he cute? I bet his little eyes and ears and nose were so cute!" Chesley persisted. Trying to impress upon her the unusual size of this creature, I said, "He was a monster, at least the size of a cat. I'm not kidding. The size of a cat. If he was smaller than a cat, I'd be surprised. He didn't run; he

SURVIVING
Hurricane Maria

lumbered. I'm not joking, he had to be almost the size of a cat." David looked at me sideways, and his expression suddenly grew grim. With his brow knit and one eyebrow slightly raised, he asked in low tones, "Wait, hold on a minute...So you're telling me he was the size of...a cat??" We all laughed until the tears rolled down our cheeks. "The size of a cat" became our preferred description of anything, large or small, from that moment on. The looks were often incredulous from our colleagues in the anatomy lab later that semester, as we would describe in our verbal reports a vertebrae or pancreas or lower esophageal sphincter as being "the size of a cat", and then snort back laughter as we tried to continue. Although our paths would separate eight months later when David and Chesley followed God's leading back to their home state of Texas, they will forever hold a special place in our hearts. To write a suitable tribute to each of the wonderful and kind friends we made on the island would fill volumes, and we are truly thankful for each one. There were my semester one anatomy lab partners, Madeleine and Nosheen, both of whom became especially dear friends of ours right away. William and his charming wife Amanda, a friendly couple we met at a neighborhood barbeque, quickly became wonderful supporters and colleagues during the study periods, and fellow-explorers during the breaks. Matthew and his lovely fiancé Courtney, with whom we enjoyed riverboat tours, hikes through the rainforests, and countless hours of pleasant, late-night conversation, became dear friends and co-adventurers. There were so many more: Kipson, Dana, Aron, Merhawitt, Ken, Cindy, Joshua, Jeri, Nicholas, Colleen, Jordan, Alysabeth...I could never begin to name them all, but we truly love and admire them, and I look forward to the honor of practicing medicine in the near future with each of these talented, brilliant, delightful people as friends and colleagues.

***

It was just a day or two before the semester began, if I recall correctly, that I received word from RUSM that I had not been selected as the recipient of the scholarship after all. I was walking across campus when the email notification chimed, "Ba-ding!" on my phone, and I came to a complete standstill on the sidewalk as I read in shocked disbelief. I had fully expected to receive that scholarship, based on my understanding of the communications from RUSM up to that point in time. I felt that there must have been some mistake. I had a letter author who had gone above and beyond reasonable expectations, taking time from his busy life to write a specially constructed letter of recommendation just for that scholarship application. I never would have asked such a thing of him, had I not been fully convinced, per the information I had been given, that I was fairly certain to be granted the scholarship. Indeed, the scholarship offer—as I perceived it—was among the primary reasons I had chosen Ross University School of Medicine from the final pool of acceptance letters. Immediately, I headed back to our apartment to discuss this turn of events with my wife. After I read the email aloud, Carmen looked at me in surprise and asked, "Seriously? Is that for real?" It was very real, it seemed. After digging back through all of the communications I had on record, I could not find a single sentence definitively stating that I would be the recipient of the scholarship. No matter how much I felt like the implication was clear, the explicit statement could not be found in any of the communications from RUSM. Suddenly, I felt like I had another decision to make. Should I reach out again to the other medical schools, or stay at RUSM and assume that it would all work out for the best? Carmen and I talked it over and prayed about it, and unanimously agreed I should stay at RUSM. I had to acknowledge that I felt disappointed and a little let down, but I really could not place the blame on RUSM. I had simply taken it for granted that being called a "perfect candidate", and being carefully guided through the process by highly optimistic admissions counsellors, was virtual assurance that I would be the recipient. Sadly, that was not the way it turned out. I never heard who was actually granted the scholarship, though I assume that information may be somewhere online. Somehow, I felt it might be better if I did not know, so deep was my disappointment. I also never heard why I had not been chosen, but I decided not to press the issue with the university. There were other ways to pay for my education, and I was not going to let a minor setback stall my progress or ruin the great relationships I was already building with some of the wonderful RUSM faculty. I sat down at my computer, pulled up the email, took a deep breath, and hit "Reply." Offering my congratulations to the unidentified recipient, I thanked the faculty for considering my application and tried to put it from my mind. Sometime in the next week, I received a notification that provided some small comfort: I was informed that qualifying candidates who failed to be selected for the full scholarship were being awarded a $500 "Book Scholarship", which would be applied to my account toward my semester's tuition.

***

My pulse quickened and my breath caught a little in my throat as I walked in. The room was enormous. There were more than four-hundred medical students in the in-coming class of September 2016, but it seemed like twice that many were seated in the auditorium assigned for

SURVIVING
Hurricane Maria

day one of orientation. Finding a seat close to a couple of new acquaintances, I glanced around the room, scanning the sea of faces. Like me, many of them appeared to be hopeful, excited, and eager to begin. We all knew medical school was going to be challenging, but we were ready to give it our best. I felt a little old, looking at my new classmates who appeared to range from five to ten years younger than me, on average, and I knew I would be required to give it everything I had just to keep up with this group of bright, enthusiastic future-doctors.

***

Attending medical school is often described as "drinking from a fire hose", and I feel like that would be a fair analogy if fire hoses were at least ten times larger than they are. There is, therefore, no equivalency or analogy that seems to fairly represent the intensity of the first semester of medical school. I am not saying that the first semester is the hardest, because it is not, in my opinion. The first semester is merely the most shocking, because most incoming medical students believe they have seen the worst a university can throw at them, by the time they have finished their four-year undergraduate degrees. Nothing could be further from the truth, of course. Due to this painful misconception, the step from undergraduate education to medical education is far more challenging, I believe, than the step from high school to undergraduate education. Perhaps many others are much more intellectually gifted than I am, and able to learn and assimilate information more quickly. As for me, I typically found it necessary to study twelve to eighteen hours per day, seven days a week, in order to pass my exams with reasonable scores that kept me moving forward each semester. Unfortunately, it seemed as though nearly half of the incoming students failed that first semester, though I never heard a definitive percentage or number from the university. Some of those dropped out, which is understandable under the circumstances; but most chose to return and repeat the semester, refusing to allow their dreams to be so quickly snuffed out. Those who experienced that setback, and then returned with even more determination, always held my utmost respect. Through their persistence and commitment, they were demonstrating their strength of character, which I sincerely admired.

***

The weather on the island never really changed much in the thirteen months we lived there. There were no noticeable seasonal changes, beyond a slight increase in rain during the "rainy season" of fall and early winter, and a slight decrease in rain during the "dry season" the rest of the year. The coastal temperatures fluctuated no more than approximately ten degrees Fahrenheit, ranging from the mid-seventies during the night to the mid-eighties during the day. Farther inland, away from RUSM and the coast, where the altitude was higher, the breeze was steady from the Atlantic side and the temperatures were consistently five or ten degrees cooler, on average. We joked many times about the fact that the weatherman in Dominica had the easiest job in the world—or perhaps the most boring. Each day was much like the last, with a few sudden, heavy showers of rain passing over a few times during the day, rarely lasting for more than a few minutes each, and quickly moving onward across the Caribbean Sea to make way for the brilliant sun and deep blue sky. RUSM had a series of alerts and email messages that were consistently sent out to warn of any larger storms approaching during the regular "hurricane season", if there was any likelihood the storms would impact Dominica.

Hurricane season was a period of increased tropical storm and hurricane activity in the Caribbean Sea, typically beginning in the summer and lasting until early winter. As a "leeward island" on the far southeastern corner of the Caribbean Sea, Dominica rarely saw the storms in their most severe conditions. For example, Hurricane Matthew from the 2016 hurricane season passed over Dominica in its earliest stages as a minor Tropical Storm, resulting in some mild wind and a few days of heavy rainfall that had little impact on the island. We always took seriously the emails from RUSM regarding the storms, but our level of concern about our physical safety decreased immensely after the first few storms passed harmlessly by.

***

Upon the completion of each semester, the vast majority of my colleagues would rush home to spend a few restful days with family and friends.

The breaks between semesters during the first two years at RUSM are relatively brief, averaging approximately two weeks. On the bright side, these brief breaks mean that RUSM students typically complete the first two academic years of their medical education within four or five consecutive semesters (sixteen or twenty months, respectively), depending on the track they have chosen. However, it also allows very little time to recuperate during the rigorous first-half of medical school. Due to the brief breaks, coupled with our growing love for our island home, Carmen and I decided to remain in Dominica for the duration of the portion of the medical education program that was offered in the Caribbean. Although I was

always exhausted by the end of each semester, I was also eager to get out into nature, exploring and photographing the astonishing natural beauty with Carmen as soon as final exams were completed.

Dominica is only fourteen miles wide and twenty-eight miles long, approximately, but it typically took us more than an hour to drive from one side to the other on the steep, narrow, winding roads. The first few times we rented a car and ventured out onto the roads were an experience for both of us—me as the driver, and Carmen as the white-knuckled passenger. She flatly refused to drive, happy to serve as navigator, instead, and she did a great job of reading the map. After spending the first couple of breaks exploring the island, we had actually driven on every major highway marked in yellow on our map, and we enjoyed every minute of our time taking in the tropical scenery and ocean views. Eventually, I broke down and purchased an ATV—a small four-wheeler manufactured in  China—as a simpler means of transportation around the Picard and Portsmouth area. In Dominica, ATVs are licensed and insured in the same manner as an automobile, and it is fully legal to operate them on the public roadways. We tried to avoid heading out for a ride when a rainstorm

appeared to be imminent, but the ATV provided a fun and speedy way to get to the  beach, run to the store, or head across town to meet up with friends. As much as we enjoyed a pleasant ride along the beach in the sunshine, we loved nothing more than a day in the warm, crystal-clear Caribbean Sea, swimming and diving with the thousands of colorful and friendly fish that darted playfully around the brilliant coral reefs. I spent countless hours in the water with my underwater camera, chasing schools of parrot fish, filming the spectacular underwater world of the coral reefs, and playing snorkel-tag with

Carmen amidst the millions of tiny bubbles rising from the volcanic sea floor. When we were at last too sunburned to spend another minute in the water, we would set off hiking in the shade of the rainforest canopy, searching out some new waterfall or lake or village we had not yet explored.

Places like the Emerald Pool, Scott's Head, Middleham  Falls, Salton Falls, and the Cold Sulfur Springs are forever etched in my memory—places we repeatedly visited because of our love for their unparalleled tropical beauty. Wherever we went, we were surrounded by tropical fruit and produce—bananas, mangos, avocados, pineapples, and much more—fresh and readily available along many of the trails and roadsides. The mangos were sometimes larger in size than my opened hand, and sweeter and juicier than any I had previously enjoyed. Carmen purchased an avocado at the market one day that dwarfed my favorite RUSM coffee mug so impressively I had to share a picture of it on social media. I have always been a lover of fruit; so much so that my mother used to tell about the many times in my childhood I asked for an extra serving of fruit-salad, instead of cake for dessert. Carmen was much the same way, which meant we were in perfect delight as we explored this tropical fruit wonderland.

***

The natural beauty of Dominica was remarkable, to be sure; but the lush, green landscapes, the brilliantly blue seascapes, and the endless, coconut palm beaches were not the only beautiful things on the island to be appreciated. Breaks were my opportunity to spend quality time with Carmen, talking and laughing and catching up on the months of  delayed "us" time. We capitalized on those short days to the fullest, often staying up late and rising early, trying to make use of every minute of time together. I also enjoyed the opportunity to get out and meet the wonderful locals that Carmen had learned to know during the weeks and months of each semester that I was buried in my studies. Shortly after arriving on the island, Carmen had started a small baking business—not because it made any substantial profits, but because it gave her something worthwhile to do with her extra time, and allowed her to make hosts of new friends out of her regular customers. Everywhere we went, people seemed to recognize her and love her, both for her outstanding baking skills and for her friendly, gentle personality. After living on the island for a few semesters, we began adapting to "island time", leaving early for appointments so we would have time to stop and chat with friends along the way, as the locals did. We loved them, and did not mind at all that we were learning to be a little more like them each day. On the way home from the clinic one sunny afternoon during my second semester, a friendly voice called out to me from across a low garden wall, "Hello, friend! Would you like a coconut?" Turning with a smile, I saw my neighbor, in his late seventies, high on a rickety ladder pulling coconuts from a tree in his yard. He gestured toward a large pile at the base of the ladder, insisting that I help myself. "Please, please, take all you want! The wife and I ain't gonna use that many!" he said, descending from the ladder to help me make my selection. I started to refuse, not wanting to get dirt on my dress clothes, but the sparkle in his eye was so kind, so generous, so eager to share from his wealth of coconuts, that I could not refuse. "Thank you so much, my friend!" I said, as I cradled the dirty coconuts in my arms, adding, "Please, stop by to see us anytime!" He smiled broadly at the invitation, and returned it. "Cool, man, and same to you!" he said, and I could see he meant it. The many friendships we developed with the warm, welcoming Dominican locals will always feel like a special gift from the island—a gift that we will hold close to our hearts for the rest of our lives.

***

SURVIVING
Hurricane Maria

Chapter 4:

Hurricane Maria—The Destruction and the Devastation

***

September 18, 6:45 p.m. – Carmen brought me a fresh cup of coffee and smiled as she set it on a coaster on my desk. "Looks like it's going to be a long night, I suppose?" It was a statement more than a question. After more than a  year as the spouse of a medical student, my wife was fully familiarized with my rigorous study schedule, and she knew that not even a Hurricane Watch would be enough to tear me away from my books. Besides, this was not a first; we had just received all the same kinds of warnings regarding Hurricane Irma a week earlier, but Irma had passed by to the north with little more than light wind and rain on our island of Dominica in the Caribbean Sea. Stirred from my intense focus for a moment by the sound of her voice, I nodded and thanked Carmen, and turned back to my computer. At that moment, my phone sounded off again, "Ba-ding!" Feeling annoyed at the distraction, I picked up my phone. "Another SIREN alert from campus, no doubt," I sighed. A quick glance confirmed the suspicion, but this one seemed more urgent, instructing students to immediately seek hurricane shelter if they had not already done so, and stating that campus was now under Hurricane Warning and would be closed until further notice. It was now confirmed that we were going to be hit by Hurricane Maria, which had only recently been upgraded to a Category 2 hurricane from a Tropical Storm. I pulled myself away from my desk and glanced out the window, checking on my ATV that was chained to a concrete light pole and scanning the road for neighbors who might not have received the newest message. The wind was blowing an estimated 60 mph, and the trees bowed low during the gusts, but there was little other sign that this was not just another typical Tropical Storm, as the rain lightly pelted the windows and rushed in muddy streamlets down the unpaved roadway. The six sturdy parachute cords wrapping the tarp on the ATV looked more like netting, the way they were crisscrossed in a dozen different directions, but I did not want to take any chances on destroying the machine in the wind and rain. The thoroughly roped tarp was not moving even in the gusts, at this wind speed. The parking brake was holding the ATV still, and the large chain around the front suspension control arm look like it was firmly anchoring the machine to the concrete power pole. No neighbors were visible on the roadway in either direction, so I deadbolted the door as a precautionary measure against higher gusts and went back to studying.

***

September 18, 7:30 p.m. – A tremendous crashing sound jarred me from the lecture notes I was reviewing. "What on earth was that?!" Carmen asked, leaping from the bed where she was doing some reading. By now, the wind had gained strength a bit, and gusts were flinging the trees wildly from side to side. A glance out the window revealed that an entire cluster of coconuts had been flung from a nearby tree onto the tin roof of our neighbor's home, smashing a section of the roofing and freeing the edge of the tin to be blown crazily in the wind. Feeling sorry for the damage to our friend's home, but feeling helpless to do anything about it until after the storm, we whispered a prayer of thanks that he and his wife were safely in the UK at the time, and hoped that their home would not suffer too much flooding due to rainfall. "Ba-ding!" My phone chimed for yet another incoming message. Glancing away from the storm outside, I saw the message was from David and Chesley, already back in Texas, asking about the approaching hurricane. I responded, "I think we are OK. It's just a Cat 2, right now. We have food and water, so I'm not too worried." David, unmatched in his sense of humor, immediately responded, "So it's about the size of a cat, then?" I started to laugh, and then was cut short by an intensely concussive gust of wind. The wind whistled around the eaves and whipped the powerlines in a way that made me shrink back from the window a bit, even though we were inside our reinforced concrete apartment building. The lights were flickering and the internet connection was unstable, but we had experienced such weather in Dominica during the previous hurricane season, and were still relatively unconcerned. In the days leading up to this storm, we had stocked up on enough preserved food and bottled water to last us about two weeks, in the event the power, water and internet were temporarily disconnected due to storm damage. We felt our supplies were likely excessive, but we justified the expenditure by acknowledging the fact that we could consume the food and water over the next two weeks even if there was no hurricane damage. We felt a little like Hurricane Irma was the hurricane that cried "wolf" on our island, because although it had done severe damage to neighboring islands, all our preparations and time away from studying had been wasted when Irma passed Dominica harmlessly by to the north. We felt deep compassion for Antigua-Barbuda and the other regions devastated by Irma, but I felt the pressure to continue focusing on my medical school studies and did not believe I had the time to invest in worrying about the next hurricane, Maria, headed

SURVIVING
Hurricane Maria

our way. Although concerned because we had recently been notified that Hurricane María had been upgraded once again to a Category 3 hurricane, I forced myself to keep studying, feeling relatively safe and secure in our three-story, solidly constructed, reinforced concrete apartment building. That would change in the blink of an eye, not fifteen minutes later.

***

September 18, 7:40 p.m. – I leaped from my desk, yanked the power cords to all my electronic devices from the wall, and dashed to the window with my flashlight. The power flickered severely for a few moments and then suddenly shut off, leaving our apartment complex blanketed in utter darkness in the raging storm. Moments later, our apartment's trusty generator automatically rattled to life, filling the general vicinity with the familiar odor of diesel fumes that meant we had at least a few hours of flickering electricity until the fuel ran out or the power came back on. The wind was now screaming around the building, shaking the concrete walls and bending the palm trees over double until they were nearly parallel to the ground. I decided it was time to step away from my studies and pay a little more attention to the safety of my wife, myself and our apartment. There was a little water beginning to seep in around the closed windows and door, so we grabbed some towels to wipe up the wayward drips. Feeling like we were probably taking it a little too far, but wanting to be on the safe side, we placed our electronics in plastic bags and moved everything possible up off of the floor onto the desk, chairs and other elevated furniture surfaces to protect them in the unlikely event of more serious flooding. Even though it was an inky black night outside, the exterior emergency lights glowed dimly in the sheets of pounding rain blowing sideways past the building. Checking my phone, which still had cellular service, I noticed that Hurricane Maria had quite suddenly grown massive, and was now projected to strike the island as the most powerful category of hurricane in existence—she was now a Category 5 nightmare. As I stood for a moment, at approximately 7:45pm, looking out the window in awe of the power of the prelude to a storm greater than any I had ever experienced, the full force of Hurricane Maria suddenly struck. There are no words to describe the horror of the next eight hours, but I will do my best to paint something of a picture.

***

September 18, 8:00 p.m. – The first wall of

Category 5 Hurricane Maria struck the island with the sustained blast of winds  between 160 and 180 mph, and earth-shaking gusts in excess of 200 mph. Trees and shrubs and stick-frame buildings, which had already been whipping and groaning in the wind, were instantly swept off into the night. Whole trees were instantly laid flat, or ripped from the ground and carried directly through the air out to sea. Cars were flipped. Pieces of roofs, trees, air-conditioning units, and shards of broken window glass constantly smashed against the outside of our walls, before being forced around to one side or the other

SURVIVING
Hurricane Maria

and carried off into the hellish night. Water droplets, leaves and mud were flying across our bedroom and striking me in the face, even though the exterior windows and doors were still in place. The indescribable power of the screaming wind was forcing mud to ooze in around the windows and doors, and to be blown around the room in small vortexes that swept loose papers from the desk and swung the interior doors wildly on their hinges. Our reinforced concrete walls shuddered. Our hurricane-grade doors bowed inward. Our hurricane-grade glass windows flexed and quivered in the perpetual blasting force. Pausing for a moment from mopping the flooding waves of water rolling across our kitchen and bedroom floors, Carmen calmly grabbed my hand and, above the deafening roar and building-crushing demolition of the hurricane-force winds, I called out to God for His hand over us and our dear friends on this besieged island, Dominica. I prayed for safety. In utter humility, I thanked God for this glimpse of His immeasurable strength, and asked that we and our friends be saved from the devastating power that was shredding the island. I prayed for my colleagues—that they would not have been caught outside; that they would be with their hurricane partners; that they would remain calm and not be driven to act foolishly through fear; that anyone in danger would find a way to safety immediately; that there would be no loss of life. I prayed for Dominica, an island already on the ropes, financially—that the damage of the storm would be minimized; that loss of life would be minimized in villages without the least protection from a storm of this unprecedented magnitude. I prayed that God would lead us to anyone who might need help in that moment, and in the days to come, as it was now clear that our existence on the island was going to take on many new dimensions. Shouting above the chaotic roaring and crashing

SURVIVING
Hurricane Maria

of the storm, I asked Carmen how she was feeling. She looked at me, smiled calmly and said, "God is with us and you are by my side. I'm perfectly fine." Never have I been more thankful for such a level-headed, calm, amazing wife. I, too, knew that we would be OK, whether or not we survived the storm, because God was truly with us. We grabbed our towels and buckets, and went back to mopping up the gathering pools of muddy water in an effort to save what we could of the apartment and our belongings.

***

September 18, 9:15 p.m. – As we fought to preserve the integrity of our apartment, it dawned on me that I should probably take a moment to notify our friends and family via Facebook™ that we were truly in the heart of one of the greatest storms on earth. I grabbed my phone. For some unidentified reason, the generator had quit working, so we had no power, and internet had just gone down, as well, but my phone still indicated that I had some type of weak cellular connection. I whipped out a brief message on Facebook™ and prayed the cell tower would hang on long enough for it to post:

> *"I'm attempting this update via cell tower, if any are standing. Power/Water/Internet are down. Even the generator quit. #HurricaneMaria is hammering us with unbelievable, earth-shattering wind and rain. The thunder of the wind utterly drowns the constant thunder/lightning. I do believe we are reasonably safe, but I feel deep compassion for those whose homes/livelihoods are being demolished. Prayers for Dominica and the Caribbean."*

Moments after I submitted the post, I lost cellular service, so I had no way of knowing whether the message had gotten out. From that moment forward, we were utterly isolated and cut off from the outside world. That attempted Facebook™ post would be the last form of contact we had personally with anyone off of the island until we were evacuated five days later; but do not let me get ahead of myself in the story.

***

September 18, 11:00 p.m. – We were now in full survival mode, operating on pure adrenaline. Water was now inches deep in places in our apartment, and we were scooping it up and filling as many basins of water in the shower as possible, so as to have a supply of "fresh" water for flushing toilets and washing faces after the storm, assuming we survived. Before midnight, we had mopped up more than twenty gallons from the bedroom floor alone. The windows were holding on almost miraculously, as trees and rocks and boards and tin roofs flew by, smashing against the exterior walls everywhere except directly on the windows themselves. Although it was pitch black, a few remaining battery powered emergency lights had not yet been blasted from the concrete walls outside, and the torrential floods of water from the sky was driven parallel to the ground, actually rushing down and around the windward sides of the buildings, or through any windows and doors the streams encountered. By the brilliant light of

my underwater diving flashlight, I could see only the nearest neighboring buildings between

whiteout sheets of rainfall; what I saw caused my heart to sink. Roofs were torn off. Windows were smashed out. Buildings were caving. Only the most sturdy, reinforced concrete structures seemed to be surviving at some level. Anything that was stick-frame did not seem to have a chance. Though I could not see far through the muddy, streaming window by the light of my flashlight, I could tell the damage was going to be nothing like I had ever seen before. Suddenly, as I was bracing my body against the steel, hurricane-grade front door to try to minimize its bending and flexing and keep the estimated 180-mph winds from blasting it from the door-jam, which I could see had already happened to others, there was a great gust of unfathomable force that absolutely rocked our entire concrete structure. I saw the few remaining palm trees in the area, sheltered slightly behind our neighbor's concrete building, instantly torn from the ground and flung off into the darkness of the belly of the hurricane. Over the continually shrieking blast of wind, I heard a loud and ominous cracking sound from somewhere in the bedroom. Forsaking the front door to the mercy of the deadbolt versus the hurricane, I dashed into the bedroom where I had last seen Carmen scooping water from the floor by the bucketful. In the light of the flashlight, she had a strained look on her face as she grimly pointed toward the source of the sound: A 6-foot long crack had appeared in the seam between the wall and the ceiling along the windward side of the bedroom. I shouted that we needed to move everything out of that area, as the water was now rushing through that crack in small, muddy streamlets that were even larger than those running in around the doors and windows. After securing the items to the best of our ability on the opposite side of the room, I took Carmen's hand, kissed her on the cheek, and put my arm around her shoulders for a moment. Nothing needed to be said; it was abundantly clear that if that wall succumbed to the massive power of the wind, as an exterior structural support wall, it would all be over in a heartbeat. We had nowhere to retreat and we lived on the ground-floor of our complex; if it collapsed, the two stories above us would end up right where we were standing. With an

SURVIVING
Hurricane María

exhausted-but-hopeful half-smile, Carmen squeezed my hand and calmly went back to work. We were not afraid. If we survived, we would be honored to have the opportunity to do anything we could to help sort through what was sure to be devastation all around us; if we did not survive, as Christians, we had a faith in the God of the universe that gave us a deep sense of peace, even in those horrifying moments. Whether in life or in death, we knew we would be OK.

***

September 18, 11:30 p.m. – As we worked together in the darkness, I suddenly froze–I thought I heard a new sound. I called for Carmen, asking if she heard what sounded like a cry for help, piercing through the shrieking wind. "I heard something," she said, "but I don't know if it was actually a person." Listening for a few moments more and hearing nothing else above the crashing of the storm outside, I finally turned back to my apartment-preservation efforts, feeling uncomfortable with what I thought I heard and listening as closely as possible for any additional sounds. Moments later, I heard it again—an extremely faint, but distinct sound of a female voice screaming for help, mostly drowned by the wind and the rain mercilessly pummeling the little island. "There it is again!" I called out to Carmen, and grabbing my flashlight, I ran to the door. I could faintly see my ATV, which had snapped to the end of its chain in the ferociously blasting

wind, straining at the concrete power pole and whipping about in the wind almost as if it were made of Styrofoam™, rather than steel, plastic and iron. The blazing sheets of wind-driven water were carried with such force than I could

see the nearby tree trunks—long since stripped of branches and  foliage—being further stripped even of their bark and left gleaming and white, with their bare wood exposed in the darkness. Sheets of crumpled tin and shards of broken glass were flying by on every side. I saw whole trees carried by the window ten feet in the air on the screaming wind. I knew it would be complete madness to even attempt to open the front door, and yet...what else could I do, as I listened to the continued, frantic calls for help somewhere in the darkness? I hated the cowardly feelings that cropped up and caused me to shrink back from this savage beast of a hurricane that was ferociously ravaging the hapless island that I called "home." So, it was not courage that drove me out into the storm, but a hatred for my own cowardice that seemed almost powerful enough to keep me from offering assistance that was clearly needed. Asking Carmen to brace herself against the door so we could get it shut again after I made it outside, I took my underwater diving flashlight and forced my way out the door, yanking it shut behind me. I cannot begin to describe or put into words the feelings I experienced while out in that unearthly, tree-shredding, building-flattening, car-flipping madness of Category 5 Hurricane Maria. The roar was so loud, so deafening, that even the crashing thunder from the lightning striking only a few dozen yards away was utterly drowned out by the earth-shredding wind. Flung from my feet against the concrete handrail like a rag doll, I wrapped my bare arms around the posts of the railing, my feet still helplessly blown behind me by the force of the 180-mph fury, and slowly, rail-by-rail, clawed my way over to the concrete steps outside our apartment, moving toward the faint sound of someone screaming for help.

SURVIVING
Hurricane Maria

Reaching the end of the concrete railing, there was a distance of about eight feet of open space I had to cross before I would be able to reach the wrought iron railing of the steps leading up the side of our tortured apartment building. The torrential sheets of rain, carrying sand and gravel and glass and debris, pelted my face and body, stinging severely like so many shots from a pellet gun. I wavered for a moment once again, feeling helpless in the screaming blast, as my feet trailing my body in the wind, completely unable to regain my footing on the tile floor of our front porch. My flashlight clasped firmly in my right hand, with the strap wrapped tightly around my wrist in case I dropped it, I surveyed the gap separating me from the next railing carefully. My courage flagged—I found myself justifying my cowardice a bit more, as I lay there with my already aching arms anchoring my chest to the concrete railing, feeling like I had reached an impassible roadblock. Then I heard it again—that frantic female voice crying for help. I could not tell where the cry was coming from, but I was absolutely driven; if the owner of that voice was still alive and still in need of help, I had no choice but to do what I could to try to reach her. Lowering myself to the floor to reduce wind resistance, I reached for the lip of a crack in the concrete floor to pull myself along. Missing the crack, and with a released grip on the concrete railing, I was once again flung backwards against the concrete railing that had saved me now for a second time. Determined to find the strength to fight my way forward, I dragged myself to the end of the railing once again, filled with feelings of self-doubt, but determined to never give in to cowardice. Bracing myself more firmly, I reached for the crack in the concrete again, and felt my fingers slide over the jagged edges and find a grip. In a forward leap low along the ground, I was finally able to grab the wrought iron railing on the

SURVIVING
Hurricane Maria

steps, and once again, rail-by-rail, I was able to move forward. The crushing force of the wind utterly stole my breath away, so I was forced to turn my head away from the wind and tuck my chin as closely as possible to my chest in order to be able to inhale and catch a breath. The stinging rain blinded my forward vision, but I was familiar with the steps and railing, so I kept my face away from the wind and rain as much as possible and slowly battled my way up the flights of stairs. At each level, I shined my flashlight down the front halls, but could see nothing that appeared to be a person in distress. By the time I reached the third floor, I was exhausted, soaked to the bone, and feeling physically worn out from the beating of the rain and the fury of the wind. It made me feel positively sick to realize I could no longer hear the cries for help. I shined my flashlight in all directions, hoping that if someone was nearby and needed help, the light would inspire a renewed effort to call out for assistance. However, I could hear nothing over the raging of the hurricane. After searching around for several more minutes, a wave of despair washed over me, as realized there was nothing left for me to do. Wiping the stinging rain from my eyes, and possibly a stray tear or two, I began fighting my way back down the stairs. When I finally arrived back at the first floor, there seemed to be a momentary pause in the fury of the wind. Grabbing extra straps from the ATV's rack, I quickly dragged the machine back over tightly against the concrete power pole, and strapped it directly to the pole with about six straps. I was determined to ensure the ATV was going nowhere that pole did not go. The parachute cords were shredded and the tarp was torn loose, but the damage to the ATV appeared to be minimal, so I secured it all as well as I could in the few seconds the hurricane mercifully allowed me. Turning to run the five steps back to the front door of our apartment, the full fury of the wind returned, once again sweeping me cleanly off my feet. Our neighbor's screen door flew past me, inches away, torn from its hinges. The downed power lines snaked about wildly in the wind, whipping from side-to-side and missing me by inches, at times. Desperately grasping for the edge of the concrete steps, I launched myself into the wind and was carried directly into the concrete railing for the third time, which allowed me a secure hold. Back at the front door, I beat on it several times to alert Carmen to my arrival. Working together, we opened it and closed it behind me, and just like that, I was back inside the relative safety of the apartment. I thanked God for my survival, prayed for the voice that I had been unable to locate and went directly back to work fighting the flooding of our kitchen. With streams of water running off of me after my excursion out into the storm, I only hoped I was removing more water than I was adding for the first minute or two.

***

September 19, 12:15 a.m. – With one hand bracing the front door against the relentless, beastly, smashing force of the raging storm, I held a bucket still for Carmen in the interior wind, as she wrung out towel after towel, drenched with water soaked up from the floor. More than four hours into the hurricane, the duration of the indescribable roar of the wind mingled with the constant crashing sounds of breaking glass and smashing buildings and disintegrating roofs and flying trees had begun to seem like an eternity. "How can it still be over us?!" Carmen asked, even as I numbly wondered the same thing. "The good news," I replied, speaking with more confidence than I felt, "is that when it's over, it will likely be over, since the eye has surely missed us, considering how long it has been like this." Never

SURVIVING
Hurricane Maria

have I been more mistaken, but that was something we mercifully did not know, at the time, and the misconception regarding the true size of the storm was some small solace in the horror of the hurricane. As we desperately battled against the elements forcing their way into our apartment, there was quite suddenly a calm that settled over the region around 12:15 a.m. It was not a complete calming of the storm, but ferociously devastating winds suddenly died back to angrily swirling gusts of an estimated 60-80 mph, tossing the miscellaneous piles of rubble haplessly back and forth in powerful whirlwinds and multi-directional gusts. The torrential rainfall seemed to lighten a bit, as well, allowing me to see a little farther with the beam of the flashlight. What I saw took my

breath away. Trees were flattened; roofs torn away;

windows smashed; powerlines down; foliage stripped away. Even in the small circle of light

cast by my flashlight, I could begin to sense the devastation that Dominica was facing, and I was filled with intense compassion for those weathering the storm in buildings far less sturdy than ours.

***

September 19, 12:45 a.m. – We were beginning to entertain a little hope that the storm may have actually passed over us. It had been relatively calm for about thirty minutes, with winds of only 60 to 80 mph and lighter rainfall. The hope was short-lived, however. Just as suddenly as the first wall had arrived, the second wall struck; but this time, the ferocity of the wind was blasting 180 degrees in the opposite direction. The immeasurable quantity of rubble created by the first half of the hurricane was now carried the other way, smashing and destroying what was left of the buildings and landscape. Our hearts sank. It seemed that there was little hope that our building and the other remaining structures could withstand another four hours of such horrific onslaught, especially from the opposite direction. Everything we had just been through in the first four hours, which already felt like an eternity, was only half of what we were going to experience before it was over. Laying down my towel and bucket on the bedroom floor, I called Carmen in to sit with me for a moment. We decided to stop clean-up efforts, which seemed futile at this point, and simply focus on survival and preserving our strength for whatever would come next. It seemed inevitable that the destruction would be complete. Again, we discussed the fact that neither of us felt fearful, though we recognized these might be our final moments. We were not afraid. We were simply in survival mode and focused on doing whatever needed to be done in each moment that remained. Our faith in God still gave us peace, and we trusted His plan for our lives and future. After checking the deadbolt on the front door to be sure it was still functionally holding the door in place, and after straightening the heavy curtains across the windows in case the glass broke, we crawled up onto the bed and rested. The storm raged. The building shuddered. Mud and leaves and rain flew across the room. The water deepened on the floor until it was draining out the front door over the door jam, whenever the wind was not driving it back inward. I marveled at the simple equilibrium it seemed to find so quickly, and wondered for a moment why I had spent so much time fighting it anyway, if it would self-equilibrate so nicely. Then I realized my concern was initially rooted in the fact that it was unusual to have

SURVIVING
Hurricane Maria

streams and pools of muddy water flowing through a kitchen and bedroom at any depth, which left me marveling at how quickly I had adapted and accepted the fact that I could do nothing about the pools and streams of water running through my house. With my arm around my wife, huddled on the bed in the dark bedroom, we waited and prayed. The building shook. The wind screamed. The windows bulged and rattled. The door bent and flexed. Trees, carried on the wind, smashed against the side of our apartment. Whole roofs, disintegrating in the ferocious claws of the wind, flew by overhead, torn from some demolished building upwind. We continued waiting and praying. I could not see her face in the darkness, but Carmen's hand was warm and soft, and I found myself feeling angry at the audacity of the tiny flecks of mud I could feel on her skin beneath my fingertips. These were Carmen's hands; my wife's hands. She had done nothing to deserve the mud that was being flung at her from across the room by this beastly storm, and yet I was utterly helpless, unable to do anything more to protect her from it. I have never felt so powerless in my life. Covering her hands with mine, I could only continue waiting and praying. The crack in the bedroom wall was a running stream of mud and water, but it did not widen. It did not cave. The cracked concrete wall—the only thing between us and the ultimately deadly conditions in the belly of the hurricane—stood firmly in place.

***

September 19, 4:15 a.m. – As abruptly as it all started, the thundering, crashing, raging of the hurricane ceased. The winds died down. The rain lightened. After more than eight hours of unspeakable destruction, the storm had passed. Carmen and I just sat in the darkness for a while, collecting our thoughts and hardly daring to

SURVIVING
Hurricane Maria

believe that this was actually the end of the storm...Hardly daring to believe the walls and doors and windows had held in our apartment...Hardly daring to believe that we were survivors...Hardly daring to think of the destruction that we would face with the arrival of morning light. Around 4:45 a.m., I heard some thumping outside near the generator. To my utter astonishment, investigation revealed our dear landlord and friend, Leroy, checking on the apartments and working on the generator to try to get electricity flowing so he could survey the damages. "How on earth did you get here so fast?" I asked incredulously. He gave a short chuckle—a chuckle unique to him, which no one else could reproduce—and said he rode a bicycle and ran from his house to check on us as soon as the storm let up. Within thirty minutes of the passage of the hurricane, Leroy had covered the three miles from his house in the inky blackness and utter chaos of the destroyed island to check on us, his tenants. We never really doubted it, but that confirmed that we had the best landlord and friend in Dominica. I asked him about his family and home, and he said they had lost everything. "The roof went—poof—just like that, gone right away. After that, everything else was taken away by the wind, too," he said. I told him to go be with his family, because we would be OK and I could check on the rest of the tenants; however, he would not leave until he personally checked on each apartment.

***

September 19, 6:30 a.m. – The rising sun lighted a world utterly unlike the one on which it set the previous evening. Just as it was getting light enough to see, Carmen and I finished mopping up the majority of the standing water from our floors. In total, we had removed more than thirty-five gallons of water from the bedroom floor alone, and we had given up counting when we moved on to the other rooms. As we assessed the damages, we realized the isolation was complete. We had no electricity, water, cellular service or internet. We were effectively cut off from the rest of the world. Did they even know what had happened to Dominica? We assumed they must, but we had no idea how long it might be until the rest of the world decided to come check on us. Boats were all surely sunk, the airport was surely destroyed, and the ports were surely demolished; we had absolutely no way to reach out or leave the island. The isolation was intense in a way that was staggering to a group used to the technology of 2017 western civilization. This was going to be a back-to-the-basics kind of survival for an unknown period of time. There was no time to waste. We grabbed raingear and umbrellas, packed a few medical supplies and some food into our backpacks, and set out immediately to check on our friends who lived in other locations.  The devastation surrounding us left us breathlessly in shock. Dense rainforest, once lush and green, had been reduced to a wasteland of rubble, stripped of all foliage and branches and most of the bark. The trees were little more than gleaming toothpicks, snapped like matchsticks into millions of splintered and twisted logs, and shoved by floods and wind into massive, jumbled piles of tangled debris. Roads in the destroyed towns were nearly impassible even by foot, due to the heaps of broken boards and tin roofs and broken glass and mangled vehicles that formed blockages in every direction.  We trekked miles that day, through a breathtaking world of loss and  destruction, reaching as many of our friends' places as possible, helping them sort through the wreckage and locate other people thought to be missing. The scenes were heartbreaking. The island was not just brought to its knees; it seemed utterly demolished. Infrastructure was obliterated. Many RUSM campus buildings were severely damaged; some were completely destroyed. Homes were shredded. Businesses were flattened. And yet, nearly every Dominican local we passed on the road asked us if we were OK. They had lost everything, quite possibly including family members, and still,

they were concerned and asking about our welfare. I was  truly humbled. Within hours, even amidst the rubble left by the storm, the local restaurant owners and store owners were selling and giving away food as quickly as they could, to feed the hungry and prevent the waste of their stock of supplies.

***

September 19, 1:00 p.m. – After six hours of hiking and searching for friends, we still had not located a few of them, but had been told that some had already headed to the RUSM Student Center for shelter, one of the few campus buildings that had reportedly survived the storm with relatively little damage. Upon arrival at the Student Center, we quickly located a few more friends. Stories began pouring in that broke our hearts. Many structures had lost their roofs. One friend described how her roof had gone early in the storm; being alone at the time, she spent the entire storm hidden in a small cubby hole underneath her concrete bathroom sink, fully enveloped in the chaos and fury of the hurricane. She watched as the entirety of her possessions were swept from her apartment in the blink of an eye, the moment the roof was torn from the building. Another friend who lost her roof was forced to move down a floor to a more secure apartment during the hurricane, fearing for her life if she remained exposed in her apartment as the roof began to let go. There are no words to describe how we all felt, as we hugged each other and celebrated the life of each person we found. Some wept. Some could find no tears, being exhausted and overwhelmed by shock. All were grateful to be survivors and deeply concerned about any friends and colleagues who had not yet been located. One friend, Nosheen, we found with a  group that had been forced to flee from their apartment complex as soon as the storm passed and the sun began to rise, because their ceilings had caved and their apartments were largely demolished. As I mentioned in an earlier chapter, Nosheen had become a close friend since we met in semester one as anatomy lab partners, so we invited her to come stay with us instead of sleeping on the floor of the Student Center, and she readily accepted the invitation.

***

September 19, 2:00 p.m. – As we had been previously instructed regarding emergency situations in which all communications were lost (which we had all assumed would never actually happen), there was a campus-wide roll call

SURVIVING
Hurricane Maria

scheduled for 3:00 p.m. This was intended to be an opportunity to check in and identify surviving individuals, as well as those who might be missing, such that we could organize search and rescue groups to be sure everyone was accounted for. Reminders about the meeting could only be passed among the students and faculty by word-of-mouth, as there was no other way to spread the news to anyone who might have been unaware of the predetermined meeting place. Around 2:00 p.m., we made our way to the proposed location, the St. James Classroom. The crowd grew far too large to accommodate everyone in that facility, so in subsequent days, the meeting location was changed to a large courtyard area near the Student Center.

***

September 19, 3:00 p.m. – Many of the professors were unable to make it to campus in time for the first roll call, due to the devastated condition of the roadways. The campus leadership announced that there was no known evacuation plan at this point, because there had been no communication with the outside world. Students were advised to secure all their available supplies in either the Student Center, or in an apartment they would share with friends. There was no way to know how long we would be isolated under these circumstances, so we were instructed to carefully ration food and water in a way that would make them last for at least a week or two, if possible. Then, we were encouraged to fill out the registration form, stay safe, work together, and return the following day for the next roll call. After roll call, Carmen, Nosheen and I immediately set off to collect any salvageable food, water and supplies from Nosheen's heavily damaged apartment to add to our stock. Forever

SURVIVING
Hurricane Maria

imprinted on my memory are the images of Nosheen bravely digging through the rubble that filled her apartment, searching for anything that might have escaped the savage teeth of the hurricane. We heaved aside piles of fallen ceiling plaster in search of her shoes and clothes; we dug

through heaps of debris in search of her priceless, irreplaceable study notes; we scavenged through the cupboards and shelves for anything that might be edible. Suddenly falling silent,  Nosheen stooped and carefully pulled a soaked, torn, crinkled slip of paper from the sludge on the floor. It was photo of her family. Brushing away the mud and broken glass, she held the picture delicately in the palm of her hand, gazing at the familiar faces she loved. For the first time since the storm, I saw Nosheen's eyes fill with tears.

There was nothing that could be said to heal her pain, so Carmen and I simply stood in silence, allowing our friend a moment with the soggy photo that clearly contained everything in the world she valued most. A moment later, she turned to us with a courageous, wobbly smile. "I really miss them. I guess I'll need a new picture when I see them again, though!" she said, with a soft laugh, trying to steady her shaking voice. I sincerely hoped she would see them again soon; indeed, I hoped we would all see our families and friends again soon. At that moment, however, our survival depended on our resilience, innovation and fortitude, and I was exceedingly impressed by the way Carmen and Nosheen were revealing their true strength of character. There was not a word of complaint from either of them. They willingly and eagerly stepped up to help with whatever needed to be done, whether it was lugging heavy supplies for miles in the sun, making food from our supplies to

SURVIVING
Hurricane Maria

share on campus, mucking mud and water from the  apartment floor, or bagging up the nauseating refuse scattered in the streets. They are unquestionably two of the bravest hurricane survivors I know.

***

September 19, 5:30 p.m. – When we arrived back at our apartment, we organized the food and water supplies, rationing them to last us as long as possible, allowing daily amounts that would avoid starvation and dehydration. Since looting was reportedly a growing problem in the regions surrounding the Picard/RUSM campus area, we created a few small bags of supplies which we stored by the front door so we would have something ready to immediately surrender if we were confronted by thieves. The rest of our supplies were hidden from view, which we hoped would deter any scouting looters. We then worked with Leroy, our landlord, to establish a non-potable water supply system for our apartment complex, since our backup water tank had been destroyed. We obtained three barrels, totalling about one hundred and fifty gallons, which could be refilled at the nearby river, thus providing us with a reasonable supply of water for flushing toilets and washing our bodies. It was not clean water, by any means, but it was functional at a basic level, and we were grateful. There is something about washing your face, even if using muddy river water, that truly helps you feel a little more "human", again.

***

SURVIVING
Hurricane Maria

Chapter 5:

The Disconnections and the Deliverance

***

The sleep-depravity, shock and general survival efforts made the next several days all sort of blend into one long day, in my memory. I do not think I slept more than two hours the entire time between the arrival of Hurricane Maria on Monday, September 18, until a week later on Monday, September 25, when we arrived back in the USA. The responsibility of doing my part to help coordinate the survival of Carmen, Nosheen and our friends weighed heavily. As I surveyed the incomprehensible destruction that surrounded us, the feeling was completely surreal, as though I had been disconnected from reality. In the past year, this island had become our home. These people had become our neighbors. These mountains had become my retreat. These rainforests had become my hideaways. Now, it all lay in utter ruins. There was scarcely a tree I recognized from the day before. The hillsides were naked, stripped of their green robes of banana trees and coconut palm fronds. The towns were crushed as with a massive sledge-hammer, and scattered about the barren landscape. Shredded curtains blew from the shattered windows in broken walls that stood alone on otherwise empty foundations. Was this real? Was it possible that it was just a horrible, ghastly nightmare, and it might be possible to find some way to wake up and escape from these agonizing scenes? Could this truly be the same green, tropical island that faded from our sight with the falling twilight the night before? As we wrestled with these feelings of disbelief and shock, we also wrestled with the stifling silence of blanketed isolation on an island definitively disconnected from the rest of the world. We had

SURVIVING
Hurricane Maria

no way to reach out to our families, or let them know that we were OK. In truth, we had no way of knowing for sure if they were even concerned about us. Did they know about the hurricane? We felt it surely must have been in the news, but how much was actually being reported? Did they know how completely we had been cut off? Did anyone know how serious our circumstances truly were? In our hearts, we believed the rest of the world knew and cared, but we deeply, urgently desired some type of confirmation.

***

To pass the time and facilitate smooth operations, several of our friends immediately volunteered to help organize the food supply system on campus; others set up a new-and-improved check-in and registration system for survivors; still others helped establish communications with the United States (when the satellite phones were eventually located) to initiate the evacuation process. If I had been forced to choose a group with which to be isolated in such apocalyptic desolation, I could not have come up with a much finer, more effective assembly than my RUSM colleagues. Although it took a couple of days, the RUSM satellite phones were eventually recovered, providing the first communication from the island since the hurricane. By Wednesday, there were military helicopters overhead providing security, and the emergency security teams—hired by RUSM—arrived from the United States to provide security and aid during the evacuation process. Friends such as Shany, Aly, Nick, Jonathon and many others were highly impressive in the way they self-sacrificially lept into action. Without their hard work on campus, there is no doubt the process would have been much more chaotic and time-consuming. Food rationing on campus allowed each person with a student or spouse ID

SURVIVING
Hurricane Maria

card to obtain one bottle of water, one other drink of choice (juice/tea/etc.), and one snack (pretzels/chips/cookies/etc.) per day. I should acknowledge, to the credit of those in charge of food rationing, that when a few hungry folks showed up more than one time each day, they did not appear to be turned away empty-handed. Fortunately, the weather was hot and sunny during this week, so Carmen, Nosheen and I went directly to work in the off-campus disaster relief efforts. We worked around our apartment complex, helped locals clean up their demolished neighborhoods, made food from our own supplies to share on campus, and I even had opportunity to provide some basic healthcare  for minor injuries. We generally stayed busy around the clock while waiting for our registration numbers to be called for evacuation. On Wednesday, we

were so exhausted, hot and sweaty, we took a bottle of shampoo to the Picard River and joined the locals in the cool water. The water was still slightly murky, but it was no longer the muddy mess it had been immediately after the hurricane, and

the bath/laundry day left us feeling immensely refreshed. We felt fortunate to have our health, at least. There were various injuries and illnesses among students and faculty as a result of the hurricane, but no deaths of medical students or faculty were reported, and we thanked God for that. Access to Dominican news was exceedingly limited, but I believed that was likely a good thing for campus morale, since so many Dominicans suffered much more terrible outcomes than the RUSM community. Through local friends, we heard heartbreaking stories of bodies being pulled from the rivers downstream of wiped out villages, and dozens of deaths in places like Roseau. All we could do was put an arm around their shoulders and pray for healing for their devastated lives. Working long hours with little or no sleep made the days pass by quickly. As we established a new, basic way of life on the little island, we were continually amazed at the way people pulled together and helped each other cope with the shattered environment. The sense of community on campus was refreshing, and grew stronger with each passing day that we all met for updates and roll call. I saw people hugging each other simply for the reassuring comfort of affectionate human touch. Others were passing the time by tossing a football, or studying flashcards in small circles. Many were volunteering to help with the storage and organization of supplies, as local grocery stores offered deep discounts to the campus to clear their shelves before the perishable merchandise all went to waste. Survival looked increasingly promising and the focus of the general student population began to shift by the second or third day after the hurricane. The questions began to pour in regarding the plan and timeline for evacuation. At first, the only answer from leadership was, "We don't know anything." After a few days, a security team appeared on campus, hired and deployed immediately by RUSM's company headquarters in the United States. They provided very little information regarding a specific plan, but they did offer reassurance that an evacuation operation was being implemented. The United States military also arrived within a few days to provide security and to airlift anyone with life-threatening injuries or illnesses. The first military  helicopters to arrive "chop-chop-chopped" their way into our lonely, barren skies after days of apocalyptic isolation like so many wonderful, whirling gifts from God. We were on campus participating in another roll call when they were first seen overhead, swooping in with a rush of wind and the scream of turbine engines, hovering just above the shredded palm trees. They were beacons of hope, promising rescue and a ride home. The great roar of cheers that arose from the student body was unlike any I had ever heard. It was a cheer of celebration, certainly, but dramatically intensified by the immense relief from

mounting feelings of desperation and fatigue. Friday night, September 22, the night before our group was supposed to be evacuated, Carmen, Nosheen, Madeleine (another friend mentioned in a previous chapter) and I spent the night on a blanket on a campus sidewalk, near the departure zone for evacuation. Not much sleeping occurred, but we felt the sacrifice would be worthwhile if we

did not miss our call to evacuation. Additionally, our landlord Leroy
needed a place to shelter his family, after their house and their belongings were completely demolished in the hurricane. We were told we would be allowed only a small duffle bag and a light backpack when we were called for evacuation, so we left virtually all of our belongings, including our ATV, for Leroy (a former police officer and respected community leader) to use and

distribute in the community, according to needs. I spoke with RUSM leadership about the possibility of staying to help the islanders rebuild, but they strongly urged evacuation due to liability, and I cooperated.

***

Evacuees were prioritized into groups as follows: 1) families with children/elderly/sick, 2) single females, 3) single males, and 4) married couples, couples who wished to travel together, and anyone with  pets. The first group of evacuees left the island on Thursday morning. Our group was scheduled to leave aboard a fifty-passenger ferry on Saturday, September 23, at approximately 3:15 p.m. The evacuation process seemed slow and laborious at the time, as the only available boats were small ferries and the voyage to St. Lucia was about fourteen hours, one-way. In retrospect, however, the

process was remarkably smooth and efficient, considering the limited communication and resource availability. Evacuees were numbered during a registration process, and then groups of evacuees were called to transport vehicles by number. The

transport vehicles consisted of whatever RUSM vans and service trucks were available and operational after the hurricane. After loading onto the transport vehicles, we were taken to a sort of staging area in an old warehouse near the Picard dock,

where we waited for the arrival of the evacuation ferry. On the ride to the dock, we passed Dominican friends who waved as we passed and called out, "Please come back, one day! We love you!" Leaving them  standing there waving goodbye amidst the scattered, shattered rubble of their homes and livelihoods was a heartrending image I will carry with me for life. It seemed so unfair that we had a safe place waiting on us—a place with plenty of food and a roof over our heads—and these kind friends of ours were left with absolutely nothing.

***

The security team and the United States military did an excellent job maintaining a safe, secure environment for evacuation. As soon as we left the port, we passed several Navy warships and other vessels

providing security and aid in the vicinity. Most of the way to St. Lucia, military helicopters could be seen and/or heard overhead, presumably ensuring our safe passage. The ferry that carried us from Dominica was a small catamaran that was

certainly not built to be an ocean-going vessel. Even though the waves were not more than four or five feet high even in the roughest places, the small boat dipped its bow into the waves and the water rolled over the deck. By that point, however, we were willing to tolerate just about anything, if it meant passage back to civilization and safety. Besides, the boat was stocked with bottled water and snacks for the trip; we were contentedly munching on peanuts and pretzels, which at least temporarily distracted us from the very real dangers of our transportation. Our route from Dominica to St. Lucia took us directly south along the full length of the island, so we had our first look at the impact on the island in general. For those of us who knew and loved the canyons, villages, beaches and waterfalls of Dominica, it was almost more tragic than we were prepared to handle. The canyons that once held small villages full of wooden shacks appeared to be stripped bare. In some of them, there was hardly a sign of a village at all. "Where did they go?" Carmen asked incredulously, over the throbbing rumble of the ferry's diesel engines. I could hardly hold back tears as I numbly turned to look out to sea in the direction the hurricane's merciless winds had blown, contemplating the potential fate of the friendly villagers we loved. There were reportedly hundreds of acres of debris fields out on the water, and I could see a few clusters of floating logs and debris on the horizon. Were there people out there, too? Why were there no helicopters out there searching for survivors on the floating logs? Would there be any real hope in a search conducted almost a week after the hurricane? Dominica, "The Nature Island" and the crown jewel of the Caribbean, was now fading in the distance, a tattered tangle of rubble and devastation, cruelly stripped of her former pristine beauty. I sat down on the engine cover near the back of the ferry and leaned back against the rusty steel railing. Closing my eyes to shut out the painful sight of the crushed little island, I tried to remember...I remembered the towering volcanic peaks, majestically robed in green, and crowned with billowing white plumes...I remembered the magical Emerald Pool, and the lacy white waterfall that delicately kept it filled with its clear, shimmering waters...I remembered the toothy smiles of the villagers, and the sincere gratitude in their gentle eyes for the free healthcare we would occasionally provide in temporary clinics...And as I remembered, I felt a sense of peace and healing begin to wash over me. The face of Dominica may have been severely battered, but I knew the heart of Dominica was growing stronger than ever.

***

About thirty minutes into the evacuation ferry ride, the diesel motors suddenly slowed. What appeared to be a sailing pirate ship was quickly approaching directly in our path, and our captain did not seem inclined to try to outmaneuver them on our small catamaran. As the dark vessel ominously drew nearer, a crew quickly lowered a small powerboat over the side and motored toward

us. It was at this moment that our captain, chuckling at our consternation, announced the "pirate ship" was another tour boat from St. Lucia, on its way to pick up more of our

colleagues. After sharing some of our extra water and snacks for our

friends, the diesel engines in our little catamaran roared back to life and we were soon on our way again. Approximately an hour later, we passed close enough to another island that we suddenly obtained cellular service. The moment was unforgettable: after the hurricane, followed by five days of utter isolation and effectively no way to get word to or from our families, we could finally

make a call. We could send a text. We could send and receive emails.

Every phone on the boat came out immediately, and I have no doubt we nearly melted down that poor cell tower. "Ba-ding! Ba-ding! Ba-ding, Ba-ding, Ba-ding..." Our cell phones exploded with notifications. It suddenly became abundantly clear to us just how aware our friends and family really had been, and how concerned for our welfare they were the entire time since the hurricane. There were hundreds of social media notifications, emails, text messages and missed calls. Newsfeeds on social media were filled with the kind sentiments of family and friends, gravely concerned for our lives and wellbeing. The sometimes anxious, sometimes hysterical, always overjoyed sounds of excited and happy voices rang noisily from each busy cellphone. The love and concern and heartache and joy that poured from the phones into the ears and eyes and hearts on that boat could never be imagined or described. Quite simply, there are no words to describe the relief we and our families felt, hearing one another's voices once again, even if only for a moment, after such a period of unknowns and isolation. As soon as I completed a few brief phone calls to family, I posted the first message to Facebook™ since moments after Hurricane Maria struck Dominica:

> "Hello Friends&Family! We are unspeakably grateful to finally be able to report that we survived #HurricaneMaria, healthy and uninjured. After a week of survival and doing what we could to help sort the wreckage left of our island community, we are currently being evacuated by boat to another island, from which we will be flown back to Miami, FL. More info/pics will be posted, but we are currently on the rescue boat passing a standing cell tower—the first cell/internet we've had since Monday. God bless you

and we love you all. Please, remember the Dominicans whose entire island has been demolished. While we medical students are being evacuated by #RUSM and the US military, our Dominican friends face extremely challenging years ahead, as they attempt to rebuild their lives. #PrayForDominica #ThankfulToBeAlive"

***

RUSM treated us exceptionally well during the evacuation, under the circumstances. As soon as we reached St. Lucia, we were put up in an all-inclusive, five-star, luxury resort, which allowed us access to hot showers, endless buffets and Wi-Fi. A few of the paying guests at the resort looked mildly annoyed at the sudden influx of medical students, likely unaware of the circumstances that brought us there; but most of them were extremely gracious and friendly, expressing their happiness for our survival and their concern for our island home, Dominica. From the resort, we were bused to the airport and flown via privately chartered jets to Miami, FL.

The jets were comfortable, and they served us a light meal in the air, which once again helped fight off the hunger pangs we had begun to accept as normal during the week following the hurricane. Upon arrival in Miami, we were met in the terminal—even though it was 2:30 a.m.—by the Dean and Chancellor of RUSM, Dr. William Owen, who warmly welcomed us home to the United States of America. The moment was special, and we all deeply appreciated the personal act of concern for our well-being. RUSM put us up in hotels and provided shuttles and meal vouchers while we waited for them to book our flights from Miami to our final destinations. All of these evacuation costs were covered by RUSM, including overweight baggage fees and the additional expenses of traveling with spouses.

***

It was with tremendous relief that we finally arrived in Roanoke, VA, on Monday, September 25, exactly one week after Hurricane Maria. We had chosen to visit Carmen's family in Virginia, first, while awaiting word from the university regarding a new study location. Carmen's parents warmly welcomed us into their home, and treated us with the sincere love and exemplary hospitality. They graciously offered us the use of their downstairs apartment, allowing us the space and privacy to sort through the few belongings we were able to bring with us from Dominica. The items we brought did not consist of much, really—just my computer and a few changes of clothes; but we had a roof over our heads and we were indescribably thankful to be able to see and hug our family once more. As soon as we had rested a few days, we booked a flight to Washington State to see my family there. The moment we arrived, we walked straight into the waiting arms of my parents and my siblings, all of whom had gone out of their way to be in Washington State to welcome us when we arrived. They were overjoyed to see us alive and well, and the greeting was unforgettable. Although our trip west was brief, it was once again a sweet time of sharing, laughing, loving, and encouraging one another to greatness. We returned to Virginia feeling truly blessed, refreshed, and much more prepared to face the serious life challenges that lay immediately before us. One such challenge was financial, since the funds we had transferred to the National Bank of Dominica prior to the hurricane for living expenses were largely inaccessible for more than a month after leaving the island. Within the first few days in Virginia, we were able to make a few small withdrawals from various ATMs, but those resulted in expensive international fees, and then the ATM card was inexplicably deactivated after a short time. The banks in Dominica were severely damaged or destroyed like the rest of the island, so we were forced to accept that the money in our account there was potentially lost. I persistently reached out to the island banks, but there was no response for many weeks. Leroy, my friend and landlord in Dominica, was eventually able to procure unstable internet connections, and we were able to have basic communication every few days. He was kind enough to visit the bank in person, speaking with some friends of his in management, and that seemed to open the lines of communication much more effectively. More than a month after our evacuation from Dominica, I finally received a call from a manager and the

National Bank of Dominica, offering to place an order for a wire transfer from my account, if I would provide the necessary paperwork. I expressed my sincere gratitude, and most of the money was successfully transferred back into our account in the United States, with the exception of a few substantial bank fees. While material losses were high and we, like many of our colleagues, face challenging times ahead as we seek to replace necessities and relocate to continue my medical education, our friends and family in the United States have shown love and kindness to us in ways that are innumerable. They have hugged us, laughed with us, cried with us, shared their financial and physical resources with us, and blessed us in ways we never could have expected. Things can almost always be replaced; by far, we are most thankful for the preservation of our lives and health. We feel the deepest compassion for our Dominican friends who truly lost everything—homes, livelihoods, incomes (due to student evacuation), and in some cases even the lives of friends and family. Of all the horrors of the experience, the loss of life was truly the greatest. We who survived have been left struggling a bit with "survivor's guilt", perhaps, as we wrestle with a myriad of troubling questions. Whose was the voice I heard screaming for help in the midst of the hurricane? Was she saved by someone else who was nearer? How many others called for help, but could not be heard or found? How many lives were lost in those canyon villages, when they were washed out to sea in the blink of an eye? How do we help the Dominicans effectively, when the western media has rarely reported on their condition at all, and we have no money or resources left of our own to share? How do we help Dominica rebuild? How do we help our Dominican friends and our medical school colleagues get back on their feet, financially and psychologically, after the intensity of such an experience? How do we put the devastation of the hurricane far enough from our minds to continue with our education elsewhere, knowing so well the conditions in which we left our Dominican friends? How do we close our eyes at night and not hear the screaming wind, or the cracking walls, or the collapsing roofs, or the fading cries for help? Hurricane Maria has passed over and moved on; but the category 5 raging of the storm will not be quieted in our hearts and minds for many years to come. Please pray for us; but even more importantly, please pray for Dominica. Please help Dominica rebuild.

***

SURVIVING
Hurricane Maria

Dear Reader,

I sincerely hope you have been inspired and encouraged, as you have joined Carmen and me in this experience that has forever changed our lives. Thank you for your kind interest in this story, and for your love and concern for our dear friends on the little Caribbean island of Dominica. For information about the ways in which you can personally help Dominica rebuild, please feel welcome to contact me (email address below) any time. Include the subject line "Help Dominica Rebuild", and I will try to respond at my earliest opportunity.

Email: SurvivingHurricaneMaria@gmail.com

Thank you again, and best wishes!

Micah D. Renicker

SURVIVING
Hurricane María

Made in the USA
San Bernardino, CA
01 December 2017